GROSS
GUIDES
TO PSYCHOLOGY
AQA (A) A2

JEAN-MARC LAWTON
RICHARD GROSS

HODDER
EDUCATION
AN HACHETTE UK COMPANY

Picture credits

The authors and publishers would like to thank the following for the use of photographs in this volume:

Figure 1.3 © jheiberg – Fotolia; Figure 2.2 © mocker_bat – Fotolia; Figure 3.1 © Yuri Arcurs – Fotolia; Figure 3.3 © Karin Jähne – Fotolia; Figure 3.4 © Richard Bowlby; Figure 4.3 © olly – Fotolia; Figure 4.4 © David Rogers/Getty Images; Figure 5.2 © motorlka – Fotolia; Figure 6.4 © Darren Baker – Fotolia; Figure 7.1 © trevkitt – Fotolia; Figure 8.1 © Farrell Grehan/Corbis; Figure 9.2 © WILL MCINTYRE/SCIENCE PHOTO LIBRARY; Figure 9.4 © Aleksandar Jocic – Fotolia; Figure 10.3 © Crashoran – Fotolia; Figure 10.4 © Richard Saker / Rex Features; Figure 11.3 © trailfan – Fotolia; Figure 12.1 © annaia – Fotolia; Figure 12.3 © drKaczmar – Fotolia; Figure 12.4 © Nikki Zalewski – Fotolia; Figure 13.3 © Andrzej Tokarski – Fotolia; Figure 14.1 © Laurence Gough – Fotolia; Figure 14.2 © Tony Veraldi – Fotolia. Figure of open book used throughout © blackred / iStockphoto.

Every effort has been made to trace and acknowledge ownership of copyright. The publishers will be glad to make suitable arrangements with any copyright holders whom it has not been possible to contact.

Orders: please contact Bookpoint Ltd, 130 Milton Park, Abingdon, Oxon OX14 4SB. Telephone: (44) 01235 827720. Fax: (44) 01235 400454. Lines are open from 9.00 - 5.00, Monday to Saturday, with a 24 hour message answering service. You can also order through our website www.hoddereducation.co.uk

If you have any comments to make about this, or any of our other titles, please send them to educationenquiries@hodder.co.uk

British Library Cataloguing in Publication Data
A catalogue record for this title is available from the British Library

ISBN: 9781444168129

Published 2012
Impression number   10 9 8 7 6 5 4 3 2 1
Year   2016, 2015, 2014, 2013, 2012

Hachette UK's policy is to use papers that are natural, renewable and recyclable products and made from wood grown in sustainable forests. The logging and manufacturing processes are expected to conform to the environmental regulations of the country of origin.

Illustrations by Barking Dog Art
Typeset by DC Graphic Design Limited, Swanley Village, Kent.
Printed in Italy for Hodder Education, An Hachette UK Company, 338 Euston Road, London NW1 3BH by LEGO

Contents

CHAPTER 1: BIOLOGICAL RHYTHMS AND SLEEP   **2**

BIOLOGICAL RHYTHMS   2
DISRUPTION OF BIOLOGICAL RHYTHMS AND THE NATURE OF SLEEP   4
EVOLUTIONARY AND RESTORATION EXPLANATIONS OF SLEEP   6
EXPLANATIONS FOR INSOMNIA, SLEEPWALKING AND NARCOLEPSY   8

CHAPTER 2: PERCEPTION   **10**

GREGORY AND GIBSON'S THEORIES   10
DEVELOPMENT OF PERCEPTUAL ABILITIES AND INFANT AND CROSS-CULTURAL RESEARCH   12
BRUCE AND YOUNG'S THEORY OF FACE RECOGNITION   14
STUDIES AND EXPLANATIONS OF PROSOPAGNOSIA   16

CHAPTER 3: RELATIONSHIPS   **18**

FORMATION, MAINTENANCE AND DISSOLUTION OF RELATIONSHIPS   18
THE RELATIONSHIP BETWEEN SEXUAL SELECTION AND HUMAN REPRODUCTIVE BEHAVIOUR   20
SEXUAL DIFFERENCES IN PARENTAL INVESTMENT   22
INFLUENCE OF CHILDHOOD ON ADULT RELATIONSHIPS AND THE INFLUENCE OF
CULTURE ON ROMANTIC RELATIONSHIPS   24

CHAPTER 4: AGGRESSION   **26**

SOCIAL PSYCHOLOGICAL THEORIES OF AGGRESSION AND INSTITUTIONAL AGGRESSION   26
NEURAL, HORMONAL AND GENETIC FACTORS IN AGGRESSION   28
EVOLUTIONARY EXPLANATIONS INCLUDING INFIDELITY AND JEALOUSY   30
EVOLUTIONARY EXPLANATIONS OF GROUP DISPLAY   32

CHAPTER 5: EATING BEHAVIOUR   **34**

FACTORS INFLUENCING ATTITUDES TO FOOD AND EATING AND EXPLANATIONS FOR
DIETING SUCCESS OR FAILURE   34
NEURAL MECHANISMS AND EVOLUTIONARY EXPLANATIONS OF FOOD PREFERENCES   36
PSYCHOLOGICAL EXPLANATIONS OF OBESITY   38
BIOLOGICAL EXPLANATIONS OF OBESITY   40

CHAPTER 6: GENDER   **42**

KOHLBERG'S THEORY AND GENDER SCHEMA THEORY   42
THE ROLE OF HORMONES AND GENES AND EVOLUTIONARY EXPLANATIONS   44
BIOSOCIAL APPROACH AND GENDER DYSPHORIA   46
SOCIAL AND CULTURAL INFLUENCES ON GENDER ROLE   48

CHAPTER 7: INTELLIGENCE   **50**

PSYCHOMETRIC AND INFORMATION PROCESSING THEORIES   50
SIMPLE LEARNING IN ANIMALS AND INTELLIGENCE IN NON-HUMAN ANIMALS   52
EVOLUTIONARY FACTORS IN HUMAN INTELLIGENCE   54
GENETIC AND ENVIRONMENTAL FACTORS IN IQ TEST PERFORMANCE   56

CHAPTER 8: COGNITION AND DEVELOPMENT — 58

PIAGET AND VYGOTSKY'S THEORIES AND THEIR APPLICATION TO EDUCATION — 58
KOHLBERG'S THEORY OF MORALITY — 60
DEVELOPMENT OF THE CHILD'S SENSE OF SELF AND UNDERSTANDING OF OTHERS — 62
BIOLOGICAL EXPLANATIONS OF SOCIAL COGNITION — 64

CHAPTER 9: PSYCHOPATHOLOGY — 66

SCHIZOPHRENIA — 66
DEPRESSION — 68
PHOBIC DISORDERS — 70
OBSESSIVE COMPULSIVE DISORDER (OCD) — 72

CHAPTER 10: MEDIA PSYCHOLOGY — 74

EXPLANATIONS OF SOCIAL INFLUENCES AND PRO- AND ANTI-SOCIAL BEHAVIOUR — 74
HOVLAND-YALE AND THE ELABORATION LIKELIHOOD MODEL — 76
SOCIAL, PSYCHOLOGICAL AND EVOLUTIONARY EXPLANATIONS OF THE ATTRACTIVENESS OF CELEBRITY — 78
RESEARCH INTO INTENSE FANDOM — 80

CHAPTER 11: THE PSYCHOLOGY OF ADDICTIVE BEHAVIOUR — 82

MODELS OF ADDICTIVE BEHAVIOUR — 82
THE APPLICATION OF MODELS OF ADDICTION TO SMOKING AND GAMBLING — 84
RISK FACTORS IN THE DEVELOPMENT OF ADDICTION AND MEDIA INFLUENCES ON ADDICTIVE BEHAVIOUR — 86
THEORY OF PLANNED BEHAVIOUR AND TYPES OF INTERVENTION AND THEIR EFFECTIVENESS — 88

CHAPTER 12: ANOMALISTIC PSYCHOLOGY — 90

PSEUDOSCIENCE AND THE SCIENTIFIC STATUS OF PARAPSYCHOLOGY — 90
COINCIDENCE AND PROBABILITY JUDGEMENTS — 92
PERSONALITY FACTORS AND EXPLANATIONS FOR SUPERSTITION AND MAGICAL THINKING — 94
EXPLANATIONS AND RESEARCH CONCERNING PSYCHIC HEALING, OBES AND NDES AND PSYCHIC MEDIUMSHIP — 96

CHAPTER 13: PSYCHOLOGICAL RESEARCH AND SCIENTIFIC METHOD — 98

THE APPLICATION OF SCIENTIFIC METHOD IN PSYCHOLOGY — 98
DESIGNING PSYCHOLOGICAL INVESTIGATIONS — 100
DATA ANALYSIS AND REPORTING ON INVESTIGATIONS — 102

CHAPTER 14: EXAM GUIDANCE — 104

MAKING THE MOST OF EXAMINATIONS — 104
PREPARING FOR EXAMINATIONS — 106

How to use this book

This book will help you revise for your AQA (A) A2 Psychology exams. It is designed so that you can use it alongside any appropriate textbook including Richard Gross's *Psychology: The Science of Mind and Behaviour* and if you choose to do so we have included page references to material in this book where appropriate:

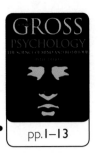

pp.1–13

Each spread covers a different topic, outlining the headline factual knowledge you need, as well as providing evaluation material to help you aim for those top marks.

Psychological research and scientific method are also covered in a colourful and exciting way to help you retain and recall the information.

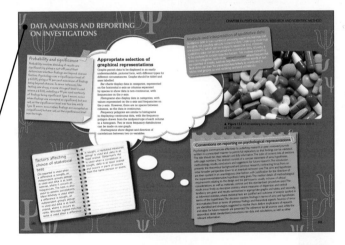

The author is a Senior Examiner for a leading exam board and at the end of the book you will find his guidance on making sure you are ready to tackle the exams!

Focal study

Czeisler et al. (1999) criticised early sleep–wake cycle studies, where participants were generally kept in isolation with no time cues, as being negatively affected by exposure to high levels of artificial light that may have continually re-set participants' internal body clocks. In their study 24 participants were kept in conditions of constant low-level light for one month with no clues as to the passage of time and were put on an artificial 28 hour sleep–wake cycle. Measurements were recorded in the form of regular body temperature readings and biochemistry levels through the analysis of blood chemicals. The findings showed that participants had adopted a sleep–wake cycle of 24 hours and 11 minutes, which differed from the earlier criticised studies that found a sleep–wake cycle closer to 25 hours. This suggests that the human sleep–wake cycle is close to the 24 hours that would logically be expected.

Description

Biological rhythms are *cyclical* behaviours that are repeated periodically. These are controlled by *endogenous pacemakers*, functioning as internal biological clocks to regulate biological functioning, and *exogenous zeitgebers* in the form of external environmental cues.

Circadian rhythms last around 24 hours, like the *sleep–wake cycle,* a free-running cycle controlled by an endogenous pacemaker operating as a body clock and facilitated by exogenous zeitgebers, like time-checks and regular meal times.

Infradian rhythms last longer than 24 hours, like the *menstrual cycle*, and are regulated by hormonal secretions and controlled by the hypothalamus operating as an endogenous pacemaker and also facilitated by exogenous zeitgebers, like pheromones.

Additional studies

- Aschoff & Weber (1962) found that participants isolated in a bunker with no natural light formed sleep–wake cycles of 25–27 hours, suggesting endogenous pacemakers control the cycle in the absence of light cues.

- Russell et al. (1980) found that female participants' menstrual cycles synchronised after a doner's underarm sweat was applied to their upper lips, suggesting that pheromones act as an exogenous zeitgeber.

- Dement & Kleitman (1957) from EEG readings found that sleep consists of stages characterised by different levels of brain activity, with dreaming occurring in REM sleep, implying sleep is an ultradian rhythm.

- Stephan & Zucker (1971) found, by removing the SCN from rats, that the usual rhythmic cycles of sleep and activity disappeared, suggesting that the SCN is the crucial endogenous pacemaker in the sleep–wake cycle.

- Luce & Segal (1966) found people in the Arctic Circle still slept seven hours nightly, even though it was continually light in the summer, suggesting that social cues act as zeitgebers to regulate sleep.

Positive evaluation

✔ Research suggests that endogenous pacemakers do exist and are regulated by exogenous zeitgebers.

✔ Turke (1984) argues that there is an evolutionary advantage to women synchronising menstrual periods, in that it allows women living together to synchronise pregnancies and thus share childcare duties. Also women working close to men have shorter menstrual cycles, giving them an evolutionary advantage in having more opportunities to get pregnant.

✔ The development of EEG readings gave psychologists an objective means of investigating sleep.

✔ There is an adaptive advantage to animals having endogenous pacemakers reset by exogenous zeitgebers, as it keeps them in tune with seasonal changes, etc.

Ultradian rhythms last less than 24 hours, like the cycle of brain activity reflected in the stages of sleep occurring through the night.

The main endogenous pacemaker involved in the circadian sleep–wake cycle is the *superchiasmatic nucleus* (SCN), a small group of cells in the hypothalamus generating a circadian rhythm reset by light entering the eyes. A rhythm is generated from several proteins interacting to form a biological clock. Exogenous zeitgebers help reset and synchronize the sleep–wake cycle, sunlight being the main one, with endogenous pacemakers responding to such zeitgebers to help regulate sleep behaviour in response to the external environment.

Negative evaluation

✘ Isolation studies of circadian rhythms have few participants, making generalisation difficult.

✘ Yamakazi et al. (2000) found that circadian rhythms persist in isolated cells from the liver and lungs grown in culture dishes without the influence of the SCN, suggesting that cells other than the SCN act as exogenous pacemakers.

✘ Findings from sleep studies are conducted in sleep laboratories with participants linked up to EEG machines, which implies findings lack ecological validity due to the artificial environment.

▲ **Figure 1.1** Ultradian rhythms last less than 24 hours, like the separate stages of sleep

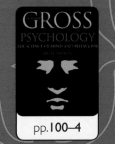

GROSS
PSYCHOLOGY
THE SCIENCE OF MIND AND BEHAVIOUR

pp.100–4

DISRUPTION OF BIOLOGICAL RHYTHMS AND THE NATURE OF SLEEP

Focal study

Cho et al. (2000) conducted research into jet lag, using 62 female participants aged between 24 and 29 years with no history of psychiatric problems. Female cabin crew from several international airlines, with a history of repeated jet lag entailing at least eight hours a week jet lag in time zones crossed, were compared to similar female ground crew with no such history, on levels of salivary cortisol – a measurement of stress hormones. Memory performance and reaction times were also recorded. Cabin crew had significantly higher cortisol levels, and cabin crew with over four years' service had poorer memory function and reaction times. This suggests that repeated jet lag is associated with high levels of chronic illness-related stress and poor physical and cognitive functioning.

Description

Disruption to biological rhythms so that they become out of step with exogenous zeitgebers can have negative consequences. Shiftwork, where people work when normally asleep, is associated with accidents and ill health, while jet lag is associated with tiredness during the day and sleeplessness at night.

Sleep is a circadian rhythm composed of an ultradian cycle of separate stages. In *stage one* alpha waves are replaced by low-voltage waves, while in *stage two* short bursts of sleep spindles occur with sharp rises and falls in k-complexes. In *stage three* sleep spindles are replaced by long, slow delta waves, which increase in *stage four* while metabolism decreases. Stage three is then re-entered, then stage two, before *REM sleep*

Additional studies

- Czeisler et al. (1982) found that shift workers had high illness rates, sleep disorders and elevated levels of stress, demonstrating the negative consequences of disrupting biological rhythms.
- Monk & Falkard (1983) found negative consequences more noticeable with rapidly rotating shifts (where shifts rotate over a short time period), than with slowly rotating shifts, suggesting that rapidly rotating shifts do not allow time for biological adjustments.
- Dement & Kleitman (1957) found that participants woken during REM sleep reported dreaming 90 per cent of the time, while only 7 per cent did when woken during non-REM sleep, which suggests REM sleep is when dreaming occurs.
- Floyd et al. (2007) reviewed around 400 sleep studies, finding that REM sleep decreased by 0.6 per cent each decade. However, the proportion of REM sleep increases from age 70, though overall sleep declined, illustrating lifespan changes in sleep.
- Van Cauter et al. (2000) found that sleep decreases during two life periods in males, at 16–25 and 35–50 years, again illustrating lifespan changes in sleep.

Positive evaluation

✔ Research into lifespan changes in sleep has led to recommendations in how infants should sleep, in order to try and reduce the incidence of **sudden infant death syndrome** (cot death).

✔ Czeisler's research in shift-workers in Utah led to the management introducing a **phase delay** system of shifts, where shifts rotate forward in time. Shift rotations were also altered to every 21 days instead of every seven days. Nine months later workers were healthier, happier and work output was up, illustrating a practical application of sleep research.

✔ Webb & Agnew (1971) found that successful strategies for coping with jet lag included outdoor pursuits, exposure to light and regular mealtimes. This illustrates how following exogenous zeitgebers is the best way to address jet lag.

is encountered where dreaming occurs, after which stages two, three and four are re-entered, with about five of these ultradian cycles occurring per night.

Lifespan changes in sleep refer to the qualitative and quantitative differences experienced at different ages. *Neonates* sleep about 16 hours a day over several periods, while *five-year-olds* have sleep brain activity similar to adults, but with more REM sleep. *Adolescents* have less REM sleep and can experience erotic dreams. In *middle age* a shallowing and shortening of sleep occurs, while in *senescence* stage 3 and 4 and REM sleep decrease, with stage 2 sleep increasing to about 60 per cent of total sleep.

Negative evaluation

✘ There has been little research into the sleep patterns of the middle-aged, as they are heavily involved with work and raising families, which suggests a full knowledge of lifespan changes has not yet been achieved.

✘ There are large individual differences in how individuals react to shiftwork and jet lag, suggesting that broad generalisations cannot be made about disruption to biological rhythms.

▲ **Figure 1.2** Air hostesses incur high levels of stress-related illness due to continual jet lag

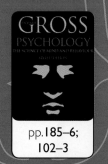

GROSS
PSYCHOLOGY
THE SCIENCE OF MIND AND BEHAVIOUR
SIXTH EDITION

pp.185–6;
102–3

EVOLUTIONARY AND RESTORATION EXPLANATIONS OF SLEEP

Description

Evolutionary explanations regard sleep as having a survival value, with different species evolving different types and patterns of sleep to suit differing environmental needs, such as predator avoidance, conservation of energy and dietary requirements. Smaller animals evolved a greater need to sleep as their metabolic rates are high and sleep helps to conserve energy, while grazing animals sleep little, as they spend long periods feeding. Predators sleep a lot, as they only need food periodically. Aquatic mammals need to breathe so have evolved sleep patterns that involve having one brain hemisphere sleep at a time, while some animals hibernate during times of food scarcity.

Restoration theory sees sleep as necessary for rejuvenation and repair. Growth hormone secreted

Additional studies

- Empson (1993) reported a general anabolic function for sleep, where REM sleep underlies brain growth, repair and memory functions, while stage 4 sleep promotes bodily growth and repair, which supports the restoration theory of sleep.
- Stern & Morgane (1974) reported that neurotransmitter levels are restored during REM sleep, supporting the restoration theory, and is further supported by the fact that antidepressants increase neurotransmitter levels, which reduces REM activity in this area.

- Mukhametov (1984) found that bottlenose dolphins have one cerebral hemisphere sleep at a time, permitting them to sleep and breathe simultaneously, supporting evolutionary explanations of sleep patterns in aquatic mammals.
- Allison & Cicchetti (1976) found that among 39 animal species, prey animals generally sleep less than predators, which goes against evolutionary theory. However, Lesku et al. (2006) points out that prey animals are usually herbivores and need long periods awake to locate and eat food. This illustrates how all relevant ecological variables need to be considered when assessing evolutionary explanations.

Positive evaluation

✔ Patients who survive drug overdoses experience prolonged increases in REM sleep, consistent with the estimated half-life of brain proteins. In a six-week period about half the brain's total protein is replaced, the approximate length of the increased REM period, which supports the restoration theory.

✔ Nocturnal secretion of growth hormone, necessary for bodily protein synthesis, depends on uninterrupted stage 4 sleep. Fibrositis sufferers have a chronic shortage of stage 4 sleep and the disturbance of stage 4 sleep in healthy volunteers produces fibrositis symptoms, adding further support to the restoration theory.

✔ The fact that sleep is universal across animal species suggests sleep does serve some adaptive purpose linked to survival.

during sleep stimulates tissue growth and facilitates protein synthesis, which repairs tissues. Oswald (1980) sees sleep as restoring biochemical and physiological processes that have been degraded during the day, with high levels of brain activity during REM sleep indicating brain restoration and hormonal activity during NREM sleep indicating physical restoration and repair. Horne's (1988) *core sleep model* believes many restorative processes like digestion occur during the day and that therefore REM and stage 4 sleep is necessary for restoration of the brain and essential for cognitive functioning, while other types of sleep are *optional sleep* whose purpose is energy conservation.

Negative evaluation

✘ Prey animals are actually more vulnerable to predators when asleep, due to decreased sensitivity to external stimuli, which implies sleep is not an adaptive response to avoid predation. Snoring while asleep is also difficult to perceive as increasing protection against predators.

✘ Oswald (1980) predicted that protein synthesis would be dependent on growth hormones secreted during the delta waves of NREM sleep, but this is not supported, as protein synthesis actually decreases rather than increases during sleep.

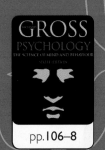

GROSS
PSYCHOLOGY
THE SCIENCE OF MIND AND BEHAVIOUR
SIXTH EDITION

pp.106–8

▲ **Figure 1.3** Predators sleep a lot as they only eat periodically

EXPLANATIONS FOR INSOMNIA, SLEEPWALKING AND NARCOLEPSY

Description

Insomnia involves problems in initiating and/or maintaining sleep, affecting both quantity and quality of sleep. *Anxiety-induced insomnia* is a *primary insomnia* resulting from stress, while *idiopathic insomnia* occurs in childhood due to abnormalities in brain mechanisms controlling the sleep–wake cycle. *Secondary insomnias* are related to psychiatric and medical disorders such as *hormonal changes* in females, *decreased melatonin production* as people age, *medical illnesses* like sleep apnoea, *mental disorders* such as depression and *lifestyle factors* such as stimulants, alcohol, environmental factors and circadian rhythm disruption. *Personality factors* such as anxious personality types and neuroticism are also associated with insomnia.

Sleepwalking refers to performing unconscious

Additional studies

- Dauvilliers *et al.* (2005) found that 72.7 per cent of primary insomniacs reported a family history of insomnia, compared to 24.1 per cent in non-insomniacs, suggesting a genetic component to the condition.
- Katz *et al.* (2002) found that 50 per cent of patients with chronic medical conditions like diabetes and depression suffered from insomnia, with 34 per cent suffering from a mild form and 16 per cent from a severe form. This supports the idea of secondary insomnia being associated with certain medical conditions.
- Chest (2001) reported a link between insomnia and obstructive sleep apnoea, implying a relationship between the two conditions.
- Bassetti (2002) found 50 per cent of sleepwalkers had a specific gene, HLA DQBI*05, which is found only in 24 per cent of non-sleepwalkers. This suggests genes may dictate the degree of vulnerability to sleepwalking.
- Dement (1999) found that mice who could not produce hypocretin in their brains developed narcoleptic symptoms, illustrating the importance of the neurotransmitter to the disorder.
- Montplaisir (2007) found decreased hypocretinergic and dopaminergic abnormalities in brainstem structures of narcoleptics, suggesting that abnormal neurotransmitter levels are related to narcolepsy.

Positive evaluation

✔ If personality is linked to insomnia, then at-risk individuals could be identified through personality testing and targeted for help and advice.

✔ Sleepwalking has been used as a successful defence in several cases of murder.

✔ Sleepwalking can be combated by using meditation and avoiding excitatory activities before bedtime. Sleeping in a calm, safe environment also helps.

✔ The drug Modafinil has proved effective against narcolepsy and works by activating hypocretin-containing nerve cells, lending further support to the hypocretin deficiency theory.

activities while asleep, like cooking food. It is most common in childhood, especially among boys and generally occurs during stage 3 and 4 sleep. It is associated with personality disorders, especially those relating to anxiety. Research reveals a genetic component, while environmental factors like alcohol, stress and medical conditions such as fever and psychiatric conditions like panic attacks are also associated with the condition.

Narcolepsy is characterised by sufferers falling asleep at unexpected times, *cataplexy*, where muscular control is lost through arousal and *sleep paralysis,* where the body is paralysed and terrifying hallucinations occur. Narcolepsy is believed to be a neurological condition associated with faulty brain mechanisms that control wakefulness and sleep. The condition appears in adolescence, as a result of a genetic abnormality. It is also associated with a shortage of the neurotransmitter hypocretin, involved in the control of wakefulness and sleep, as well as resulting from an autoimmune disease.

Negative evaluation

✘ Kellaway (2008) reports increases in insomnia are due to increased anxiety, with insomniacs 40 times more likely than non-insomniacs to be depressed. This is supported by Hill (2007) who found women are twice as likely as men to have insomnia and twice as likely to be depressed.

✘ No medical treatment such as drug therapies have yet been devised to combat sleepwalking and as the disorder incurs serious accidents and distressing incidents, such as partners having sleep sex with strangers, a successful treatment is essential.

✘ Finnish researchers report a link between swine fever vaccination and childhood narcolepsy, which suggests such vaccination has debilitating side-effects.

▲ **Figure 1.4** Sleepwalkers perform unconscious activities while asleep, like sleep cooking

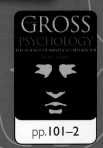

GROSS
PSYCHOLOGY
THE SCIENCE OF MIND AND BEHAVIOUR
SIXTH EDITION

pp.101–2

Focal study

Stoffregen *et al.* (1995) was influenced by the fact that most research into affordances concentrated on individuals' own actions, which invariably fail to support the concept. This research alternatively tested the affordances of the actions of others. Participants were asked to observe tall and short actors (1) standing next to an adjustable chair and (2) in motion, for example walking on the spot, to represent the dynamic action of real-life situations. From these observations participants were asked to make judgements of preferred and maximum sitting heights for each actor. In both conditions participants gave accurate judgements of preferred and maximum sitting heights, which lends support to the idea that affordances are accessible through direct perception of sensory data.

Description

Gregory saw perception as a dynamic searching for the best interpretation of available data. Sensory data is often incomplete or ambiguous and therefore individuals need to go beyond available data to make sense of it, continually generating and testing hypotheses about what is being experienced. *Perceptual set* refers to the fact that individuals are biased in their perceptions, perceiving what they expect to see based on *previous experience* and being influenced by *emotional factors* that create a bias to perceive, or not, certain features of sensory data. Individuals are influenced to perceive in certain ways due to *motivational factors*, like hunger, and by *cultural factors* that predispose people to perceive environmental features in certain ways.

Additional studies

- Solley & Haigh (1948) found that children drew pictures of a bigger Santa and sack of toys as Christmas approached and then smaller ones after Christmas had passed, which suggests motivation influences perception in line with Gibson's theory.
- Leeper (1935) found that participants previously given a picture of a young woman perceived a young woman in an ambiguous figure perceivable as either an old or young woman, while those previously shown a picture of an old woman perceived an old woman in the ambiguous figure. This suggests expectation influences perception in line with Gregory's theory.
- Gibson & Bridgeman (1987) found that participants correctly identified objects, their colour and spatial whereabouts, etc., from photographs of surface textures, supporting Gibson's idea that perception is directly experienced from sensory data.
- Maher & West (1993) found that animal species were identifiable from films of them in motion, clad in black with lights on their joints. This illustrates that there is sufficient information in the optic array to perceive directly, supporting Gibson.

Positive evaluation

✔ Gregory and Gibson's theories can be combined to give a fuller account of perception. Gibson's direct theory works best when sensory data is sufficiently rich and viewing conditions ideal, while Gregory's indirect theory explains those occasions when we have to go beyond sensory data as it is impoverished.

✔ Gibson's theory has several practical applications. Gaver (1996) applied the concept of affordances to designing computer displays, while traffic accidents have declined due to putting parallel lines closer together as road junctions approach, which gives a false impression of speed, causing drivers to slow down.

Gibson however sees sensory data as being rich enough to perceive directly from, and believed perception occurred due to the direct detection of *environmental invariances* –unchanging features of the environment that exist within the *optical array*, the ever-changing patterned light that hits the eyes. *Optic flow patterns* are unambiguous sources of information about height, distance and speed that directly inform perception, *texture gradient* concerns surface patterns that inform about depth, shape etc., of objects, while *horizon ratios* concern the position of objects in relation to the horizon and *affordances* concern the quality of objects that permit actions to be carried out on them, for example a comb 'affords' the combing of hair.

Negative evaluation

✗ The notion of affordances permitting perception of what objects can do being directly accessible from the optical array seems unlikely, as such knowledge is generally gained from experience and cultural influences, for instance that a hair drier is for drying hair.

✗ Much research supporting Gregory is laboratory-based and uses artificial, biased scenarios that deliberately restrict sensory data so that it would be impossible to perceive directly from it. Real-life environments generally provided much richer levels of sensory data from which direct perception may be possible.

▲ **Figure 2.1** Children draw increasingly bigger pictures of Santa and toys as Christmas approaches

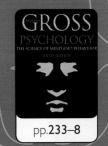

GROSS
PSYCHOLOGY
THE SCIENCE OF MIND AND BEHAVIOUR
SIXTH EDITION

pp.233–8

DEVELOPMENT OF PERCEPTUAL ABILITIES AND INFANT AND CROSS-CULTURAL RESEARCH

Focal study

Gibson & Walk (1960) tested whether depth perception was innate or learned by constructing an apparatus, covered with non-reflective glass, which had an apparent vertical drop. As neonates cannot crawl, 36 children aged between 6 and 14 months were used. The children's mothers called to their infants to come to them, an action which required crawling over the apparent vertical drop. Only three children (8 per cent) crawled over the cliff; indeed many others crawled away from their mothers and the vertical drop, while others remained still and cried. Vision was evidently important, as many children peered down through the glass before backing away. The findings suggest that depth perception is more innate than learned.

Description

Perception consists of several abilities, some learned, while others are innate. Innate perceptual abilities have an immediate survival value, allowing neonates to interact with their environment, while learned abilities allow individuals to adapt to different perceptual environments. *Depth* and *distance* perception permit the experience of the environment as three-dimensional, helping individuals to move around and interact with their environment. Because all of an object cannot be seen at once, *visual constancies* allow them to appear unchanging, regardless of the viewing conditions, creating a sense of a predictable environment that is easier to deal with.

Neonate studies allow us to see which perceptual abilities are present at birth and thus are innate,

Additional studies

- Campos et al. (1994) found that 9–12-month-olds would not cross an apparent vertical drop if their calling mothers simulated fear, but would if they simulated encouragement, which suggests that infants use learned non-verbal cues to confirm or override their innate depth perception.
- Montello (2006) performed a meta-analysis of cross-cultural studies of depth and distance perception, finding cultural differences to be small, which suggests perceptual abilities are innate and have evolved due to their survival value.

- Bower (1966) conditioned 2-month-olds to turn their heads to a 30 cm cube at one metre away. Various cubes of differing sizes and at differing distances were then presented. The participants mainly responded to the original conditioned stimulus, suggesting that size constancy is innate.
- Turnbull (1961) reported that a pygmy with no experience of long-distance environments thought that, when taken to the wide open spaces of the savannah grasslands, a distant herd of buffalo were insects, suggesting that the depth cues necessary for distance perception are learned.

Positive evaluation

✔ Both neonate and cross-cultural studies permit scientific exploration of the nature versus nurture debate. This has allowed psychologists to discover that basic perceptual skills, with their inherent survival value, are more a product of nature, whereas elaborate perceptual skills that permit adaptation to changing environments require learning experiences and are thus more of a product of nurture.

✔ Research into the development of perceptual abilities has practical applications, such as the development of computer technologies that reflect the perceptual abilities of humans of different ages.

though some innate abilities may not be immediately apparent, as they require time to mature. Studies suggest that depth and distance perception tend to be innate, though more sophisticated forms require learning experiences, while visual constancies, such as shape, size, colour and brightness constancies differ in the degree to which they are innate depending on which sensory mode they occur through.

Cross-cultural studies also permit an assessment of the *nature versus nurture debate*. If people from different cultures living in different environmental worlds have similar perceptual abilities, then it suggests they are innate, whereas if they have different perceptual abilities it indicates they are learned. This is often achieved by seeing if people of different cultures experience visual illusions differently.

Negative evaluation

✗ With Gibson & Walk's study it is not certain that depth perception is innate, as babies need to be old enough to crawl to be tested, by which time they have had learning experiences. However, studies with animal species that can move at birth suggest the ability to be innate.

✗ Neonate studies that distress infants, such as encouraging them to crawl over an apparent drop, may be considered to be unethical.

✗ Cross-cultural research tends to focus on visual illusions and 2D drawings, which may not relate to everyday life and therefore lack ecological validity.

▲ **Figure 2.2** Neonate studies allow psychologists to see whether perceptual skills are innate or not

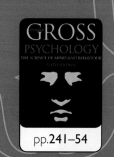

GROSS PSYCHOLOGY
THE SCIENCE OF MIND AND BEHAVIOUR
SIXTH EDITION

pp.241–54

13

BRUCE AND YOUNG'S THEORY OF FACE RECOGNITION

Description

Bruce & Young's stage theory sees two types of information held about individuals to help recognise familiar faces: (i) *visually derived semantic code*, which holds details directly related to physical aspects, like gender, and (ii) *identity-specific semantic code*, which holds biographical details not related to physical aspects, like hobbies. Face recognition involves eight independent processing modules working in sequential fashion:

1. *Structural encoding*, concerning the creation of descriptions and representations of faces.

2. *Expression analysis*, concerning the analysis of facial characteristics to infer emotional state.

3. *Facial speech analysis*, concerning the analysis of facial movements to comprehend speech.

Additional studies

- Tanaka & Farah (19993) found that facial features learned in the context of a normal upright face were more likely to be identified when viewed collectively than in isolation, though this was not true for inverted faces. This suggests the representation of whole faces is based on a holistic description, while inverted faces are represented as a set of independent components.

- Bradshaw & Wallace (1971) presented pairs of faces to participants and found that the more differences there were between a pair of faces, then the faster participants responded. This implies that facial features are processed independently and sequentially.

- Sergent (1984) constructed eight slightly different faces constructed from the same facial features, but each with one of two chins, eye colours and arrangement of internal features. Pairs of 'different' faces were intermixed with pairs of identical faces, with participants having to decide whether 'different' pairs were different or identical. When only a single feature differed, 'difference' decisions were quicker when involving chins and when something in addition to chins differed, decisions were even quicker. This suggests there is interactive processing of different dimensions of facial appearance.

Positive evaluation

✔ Bruce & Young's (1986) theory allowed predictions to be made, which research supported as true. The idea that familiar and unfamiliar faces are processed differently was supported by evidence and the idea that the processing of facial information occurring in sequential fashion was also supported.

✔ Research studies of visual agnosias, where sufferers cannot make sense of some visual information, have provided additional support for Bruce & Young's notion that face recognition consists of independent sub-components.

✔ The central concept that face recognition is a holistic process, comprising a set of independent stages, is also generally supported by research, giving the theory additional support.

4. *Directed visual processing*, concerning selective processing of specific data, like the shape of eyes.

5. *Facial recognition nodes* (FRNs), concerning stored structural descriptions of familiar faces.

6. *Person identity nodes* (PINs), concerning stored information about familiar people, like their hobbies.

7. *Name generation*, concerning a separate store for names.

8. *Cognitive storage*, concerning additional information assisting recognition, like the context a person is known in.

Recognising familiar faces involves matching structural information describing familiar faces stored in the FRNs, using facial features and their configuration to accomplish this. Identity-specific information is then accessed from the PINs, permitting specific names and biographical details to be accessed. Recognising unfamiliar faces involves the use of structural encoding, expression analysis, facial speech analysis and directed visual processing.

▲ **Figure 2.3** Bruce & Young believe that face recognition involves eight independent processing modules working in sequential fashion

Negative evaluation

✘ The relationship between face and object recognition is not fully understood, especially if they are processed separately using different mechanisms.

✘ Research mainly uses static pictures rather than the dynamic faces of real life and therefore may not reflect how face recognition really happens.

✘ It is not understood how some components work, for example cognitive storage, therefore leaving the theory incomplete.

GROSS
PSYCHOLOGY
THE SCIENCE OF MIND AND BEHAVIOUR

pp.215–16

STUDIES AND EXPLANATIONS OF PROSOPAGNOSIA

Focal study

Delvenne *et al.* (2003) investigated the visual processes of a patient referred to as NS, who at age 40 was hit by a car, incurring damage to his bilateral occipito-temporal junction area, leaving him with a severe visual agnosia for objects and faces. NS was given a battery of perceptual tests, including drawing objects, matching objects and faces and computer-based perceptual tests. It was found that NS had perfect visual abilities, except for tasks requiring access to visual semantic knowledge, like naming familiar objects. With faces NS could identify individual features, read emotion, etc., but could not assess whether a face was familiar. His deficit was in being able to process objects as a whole. It was concluded that prosopagnosia involves a deficit in the perception of high-level visual processes necessary to correctly identify familiar faces.

Description

Visual agnosias, of which prosopagnosia is a type, involve sufferers having undamaged visual systems but being unable to make sense of certain visual information. Damage to the posterior occipital and/or the temporal lobes of the brain appear to be the main cause of the disorder, though there is a congenital type that occurs without brain damage. Sufferers can describe faces and objects in terms of features and colours, etc., but cannot name them, even if they are familiar. There are two types: (1) *apperceptive,* involving an inability to recognise familiar faces and objects, though vision is unaffected, and (2) *associative,* involving an inability to recognise familiar objects through loss of access

Additional studies

- Brunsdon *et al.* (2006) reported on AL, a boy unable to recognise familiar or unfamiliar faces, suggesting damage was at the level of structural encoding at the beginning of the face recognition process. This supports Bruce & Young's idea that face recognition occurs through sequential stages.

- Bruyer *et al.* (1983) had a patient who could understand facial expressions but could not name them, while Kurucz *et al.* (1979) reported on several prosopagnosics with opposite symptoms who could name facial expressions, but could not understand them. This suggests that facial expression analysis and

name generation are separate components of face recognition in line with Bruce & Young's theory.

- Campbell *et al.* (1986) reported on a prosopagnosic who could not name familiar faces, nor identify facial expressions, but could perform speech analysis, suggesting that facial speech analysis is a separate component of face recognition.

- Bodamer (1947) coined the term prosopagnosia. He reported on one case where a man with a bullet wound to the head could not recognise familiar faces or his own mirror image. But he could recognise people using other senses, such as smell, which implies only his visual processing was affected.

Positive evaluation

✔ Case studies of prosopagnosia have allowed psychologists to understand that as the disorder affects face recognition in different ways, face recognition occurs as a holistic process of sequential, independent sub-components.

✔ Studies of prosopagnosics have benefited sufferers, as it is now known that the condition does not involve mental retardation and that indeed prosopagnosics can live relatively normal lives, for example NS worked full-time as a laboratory researcher.

to stored semantic information. Perception of faces and objects was originally believed to be processed by the same neural mechanisms, but case studies of prosopagnosia indicate two separate systems, with a specific processing mechanism for faces. With prosopagnosia damage is specific to the *fusiform gyrus* brain area, objects being recognisable, but not faces. There are different types and levels of prosopagnosia affecting different modules of face recognition, which supports Bruce & Young's idea of face recognition occurring as a sequence of stages and suggests that each face-processing module involves a different brain area. Damage to these different areas leads to the different types and levels of prosopagnosia.

Negative evaluation

✘ Case studies of prosopagnosia are performed upon individuals with abnormal brain conditions and so may not be representative of how face recognition occurs in non-damaged people.

✘ Gauthier et al. (2000) argues that face recognition may not involve separate processing mechanisms, because in perceptual terms faces may just be objects that are so complex they take more processing to recognise. This idea is supported by the fact that the fusiform gyrus is activated during both face and object recognition. This is further supported by some prosopagnosics also having problems recognising complex objects.

Fusiform

▲ **Figure 2.4** Prosopagnosia involves damage to the fusiform gyrus brain area

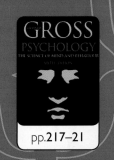

GROSS
PSYCHOLOGY
THE SCIENCE OF MIND AND BEHAVIOUR
SIXTH EDITION

pp.217–21

FORMATION, MAINTENANCE AND DISSOLUTION OF RELATIONSHIPS

Focal study

Yum et al. (2009) assessed whether the role of equity in relationship maintenance was a cross-cultural phenomenon. Most research had previously occurred in western cultures and therefore findings were not generalisable to other countries with different cultural viewpoints regarding relationships. Therefore the researchers here looked at heterosexual romantic relationships in six countries: USA, Spain, Japan, China, South Korea and the Czech Republic. Participants completed self-assessments of equity and recent relational maintenance strategy use. Differing cultural values were also considered. As predicted by equity theory, maintenance strategies varied, with individuals in perceived equitable relationships engaging in most maintenance strategies, followed by those in perceived over-benefited and under-benefited relationships. Cultural factors had little effect, suggesting that equity theory can be applied cross-culturally.

Description

The *sociobiological theory* of relationship formation is an evolutionary theory with males seeking to further their genes through multiple partners and signs of fertility, while females seek resource-rich, genetically strong males.

The *reinforcement and needs satisfaction theory* is a behaviourist theory of relationship formation based on conditioning where reinforcement through provision of companionship, love and sex increases chances of relationships forming.

The *social exchange theory* sees people as selfish, with individuals viewing their regard for partners in terms of profits. Therefore the greater the rewards and the lower the costs, the greater the desire to maintain a relationship.

Equity theory perceives individuals as motivated to achieve fairness, therefore relationships are maintained by establishing balance and stability,

Additional studies

- Davis (1990) examined personal advertisements, finding that men seek health and attractiveness and offer wealth and resources, while women seek resources and status, while offering beauty and youth, thus supporting the sociobiological theory.
- Griffit & Veitch (1971) reported that evaluations of strangers were positive when evaluations were made in a comfortable environment. This supports the reinforcement and needs satisfaction belief that conditioning through association explains relationship formation.
- Rusbult (1983) found that the rewards and costs of current relationships were compared to the rewards and costs of potential alternative relationships in order to decide whether to maintain relationships, supporting the social exchange theory of maintenance.
- Argyle (1988) reported that females blamed dissolution on a lack of emotional support, while men blamed a lack of fun, which suggests there are gender differences in relationship breakdown that Duck's theory does not consider.
- Lee (1984) reported that individuals who missed out some stages of dissolution, going straight instead to the termination phase, were those with less intimate relationships, while those who proceeded through the stages in a lengthy fashion still felt attracted to ex-partners and had greater feelings of loss and loneliness.

where partners should be putting as much into a relationship as they get out of it. The recognition of inequity in relationships provides an opportunity for relationships to be saved. *Duck's theory of relationship dissolution* sees relationships breaking down in set phases, where partners move from perceiving dissatisfaction to establishing a post-relationship view of the breakdown that protects self-esteem and rebuilds life towards new relationships. *Lee's model of relationship dissolution* is a five-stage model, similar to Duck's, that perceives breakdown as a process occurring over time, which takes partners from dissatisfaction through to break-up and includes attempts to resolve dissatisfaction so that relationships can be saved.

GROSS
PSYCHOLOGY
THE SCIENCE OF MIND AND BEHAVIOUR

pp.**434–44**

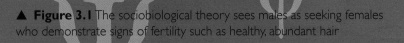

▲ **Figure 3.1** The sociobiological theory sees males as seeking females who demonstrate signs of fertility such as healthy, abundant hair

THE RELATIONSHIP BETWEEN SEXUAL SELECTION AND HUMAN REPRODUCTIVE BEHAVIOUR

Focal study

Simmons *et al.* (2003) researched into a possible relationship between human testes size and sexual behaviour, as predicted by evolutionary theory. A questionnaire on lifetime sexual behaviour, including non-partner sex, was completed by 194 female and 222 Australian males. Males gave self-measurements of testes size and 50 provided sperm samples after 48 hours abstinence from sex, with seven males producing four samples to assess reliability. There was no gender differences in extra-pair copulations and testes size was positively correlated with sperm production, in line with evolutionary theory. However, there was no association between testes size and amount of extra-pair copulations, which lessens the support for evolutionary predictions.

Description

Evolutionary theory sees differences in male and female sexual behaviour as having arisen due to different selective pressures. Males are not certain of paternity, so their best strategy to maximise chances of reproduction and the passing on of genes is to impregnate as many females as possible. This bears little reproductive cost to males as they produce vast amounts of sperm. Males therefore seek signs of fertility in women, such as youth, healthiness and childbearing hips, and indulge in intrasexual competition with other males to gain access to high-quality females. Females are certain of maternity, but produce relatively few eggs, so reproductive activity has a greater cost for them than males. Their best strategy is to indulge in intersexual competition

Additional studies

- Cartwright (2000) found that females with symmetrical breasts were more fertile than those with non-symmetrical breasts, which suggests that body symmetry is indicative of reproductive fitness. This was supported by Penton-Voak *et al.* (2001) which found that females select males with greater facial symmetry.

- Partridge (1980) forcibly mated some female fruit flies with randomly selected males, while others were permitted a free choice. It was found that the offspring of the free-choice matings had greater competitive ability, implying that females increase their reproductive success by selecting partners of good genetic quality.

- Buss (1989) found that males in 37 different cultures preferred young, healthy, physically attractive females, while females preferred resource-rich, ambitious, hard-working males. This supports the idea of gender-based differences in sexual selection in line with evolutionary theory.

- Singh (1993), using data from beauty pageants and *Playboy* centrefolds, found that there was a consistent preference by males for females with a waist-to-hip ratio of 0.7:1. Swami & Furnham (2006) assessed that supermodels corresponded closely to this, supporting the idea of childbearing hips being an attractive feature in females.

Positive evaluation

✔ Females often manipulate their appearance through cosmetics and surgery, as well as lying about their age, in order to appear younger and more fertile. Males will often exaggerate their resource richness and feign being in love to get females to mate with them, all of which support evolutionary predictions of human sexual behaviour.

✔ Evolutionary predictions about sexual behaviour and reproduction strategies are generally found to be true for all animal species, with variations in behaviour between different species understandable by reference to differences in environmental pressures. This supports the notion that differences in sexual behaviour are evolved ones.

and select the fittest males to produce healthy children that are better able to survive to sexual maturity. The female therefore seeks wealth and resources in males: indicators that they will be able to provide for her and her children. Females also get males to spend time, effort and resources in courting them, in order to reduce the chances of males deserting and leaving childcare solely to females and taking their resources elsewhere. Males indulge in courtship rituals to compete and display genetic potential and have also evolved to be bigger in order to compete with other males. Both males and females benefit from copulation with non-partners; males by increasing chances of reproductive success and females by widening the genetic diversity of their children, thereby increasing their survival chances.

Negative evaluation

✗ It is difficult to separate the effects of sexual selection from natural selection, making research difficult.

✗ Evolutionary theory does not really explain romantic relationships where individuals choose not to have children, or homosexual relationships that cannot result in pregnancy.

✗ Human and chimpanzee males often prefer substantially older females, which does not fit evolutionary theory, as they are less fertile, although it is possible they are preferred due to their proven fertility and maternity.

▲ **Figure 3.2** Females manipulate their appearance, such as with cosmetics, to appear younger and thus more fertile

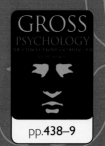

GROSS
PSYCHOLOGY

pp.438–9

SEXUAL DIFFERENCES IN PARENTAL INVESTMENT

Description

Parental investment (PI) concerns investment by parents into individual offspring, increasing their chances of survival to sexual maturity, at the expense of investing in other offspring. PI therefore involves the provision of resources, like food, protection, etc. Gender differences exist in PI, with females making a bigger initial investment because eggs are more costly to produce than sperm and females bear the costs of carrying the developing foetus and breastfeeding. Females cannot reproduce while pregnant, whereas males are not similarly constrained. Low-investing males have sufficient resources to produce many offspring and favour a quantity over quality approach, impregnating as many females as possible. High-investing females favour quality over quantity, being choosier with

Additional studies

- Gross & Shine (1981) reported that parental care by males occurred in 70 per cent of animal species, but in 86 per cent of species by females, supporting evolutionary predictions of gender differences in PI.
- Dawkins & Carlisle (1976) found that males provide sole parental care in 35 out of 46 species where there is simultaneous gamete release, which refutes the predictions of evolutionary theory.
- Daly (1979) reported that monogamy and bi-parental care was generally found in mammal and bird species where offspring require intensive, resource-rich rearing, supporting evolutionary predictions of PI.
- Brase (2006) found that males who demonstrated a positive attitude towards PI were more attractive as sexual partners to females, which again supports evolutionary predictions.
- Krebs & Davies (1981) found that in fish species where males produce sperm into a nest first, followed by females releasing eggs, the males provide sole parental care, even though males have the first opportunity to desert. This goes against the predictions of evolutionary theory concerning PI.

Positive evaluation

✔ Some see evolutionary theory as redundant as it is impossible to falsify. However, the theory can be tested by assessing if evolutionary predictions concerning PI are actually true in real-world settings.

✔ Some evidence seemingly refuting evolutionary theory is explicable in evolutionary terms. **Neonaticide**, the murder of neonates by mothers, seems initially to go against the evolutionary idea of maximising reproductive success. However, in conditions of poverty it may have an adaptive value. Stone et al. (2005) found that younger mothers commit neonaticide more than older mothers, as they have more chance of replacing such offspring and that neonaticide occurs more when a mother's chances of supporting a child are severely compromised.

whom they mate. Males compete against each other in *intrasexual* competition for access to females, while females choose from available males in *intersexual* competition. Evolutionary theory predicts how male and female PI will differ:

1. *Parental certainty*, where males are likelier to desert with internal rather than external fertilisation, as they are less sure of paternity.

2. *Order of gamete release*, where internal fertilisation gives males first chance of deserting, while external fertilisation gives females first chance.

3. *Monogamy*, where exclusive pair bonds form if childcare is intensive.

4. *Grandparental certainty*, where more resources come from maternal grandparents, as they have greater certainty of genetic relatedness.

Negative evaluation

✗ As predicted by evolutionary theory, children are 60 times likelier to be murdered by a step-parent than a biological one, as they are not genetically related. However, most step-parents invest heavily in step-children and do not harm them, which refutes evolutionary theory.

✗ Evolutionary theory predicts that fathers should invest more in children than step-fathers, but Andersson et al. (1999) found that generally investments in the college education of children was equal between fathers and step-fathers.

▲ **Figure 3.3** In species with external fertilisation females have first opportunity to desert

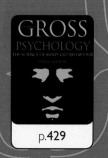

GROSS
PSYCHOLOGY
THE SCIENCE OF MIND AND BEHAVIOUR
SIXTH EDITION

p.429

INFLUENCE OF CHILDHOOD ON ADULT RELATIONSHIPS AND THE INFLUENCE OF CULTURE ON ROMANTIC RELATIONSHIPS

Focal study

Hazan & Shaver (1987) assessed possible links between childhood attachment and adult romantic relationships. Participants responded to a 'love quiz' in a newspaper, selecting one of three descriptions that reflected a secure, an insecure-resistant or an insecure-avoidant attachment type, and which reflected their feelings of adult romance. Participants also completed a checklist relating to childhood relationships with parents. Those identified with childhood secure attachments had positive perceptions of adult relationships and longer lasting relationships. Those with insecure-resistant attachments doubted the existence of romantic love and its essentialness to happiness. Those with insecure-avoidant attachments had more self-doubts and, as with insecure attachments, increased loneliness. It was concluded that childhood attachment types are positively correlated with childhood attachment experiences.

Description

Researchers have attempted to assess whether the *quality* and *type* of relationships people have in adulthood is related to childhood experiences. Bowlby (1951) proposed the *continuity hypothesis*, where attachments made with primary caregivers in infancy provided an *internal working model* acting as a template for future adult relationships. Attachment style is seen as providing children with a set of beliefs about themselves and others and about the nature of relationships. It is thought that attachment types predict adult relationships, for instance that someone with a secure attachment in childhood will go on to have intimate, secure adult relationships, while those with insecure attachments will not. Hazan & Shaver (1987) proposed that early attachment patterns affect *romantic relationships, caregiving* and *sexuality* in adulthood.

Additional studies

- Van Ijzendoorn & Bakermans-Kranenburg (1996) found that securely attached males gave more emotional support, more reassuring comments and displayed greater concern for partners than insecurely attached males, which suggests that those with secure attachments are more skilled in developing and maintaining intimate relationships.

- Le Vine et al. (1993) found that participants from collectivist cultures were more likely than those from individualist cultures to marry someone they did not love, but had other qualities desirable in a marriage, supporting the notion that people from traditionalist cultures marry for reasons other than love.

- McHenry & Price (1995) reported that divorce rates had risen in traditionalist cultures where females had gained more independence and influence, suggesting that the low rates of divorce in such cultures is not reflective of contentment in marriage, but of male dominance over females.

- Gupta & Singh (1982) assessed couples after one, five and ten years of marriage, finding that in voluntary love marriages loving and liking were initially high, but decreased over time, while those in arranged marriages increased loving and liking over time, which suggests arranged marriages are more successful over time and reflect the benefit of parental advice concerning compatibility.

Positive evaluation

✔ Research suggests that insecurely attached individuals are not doomed to be unsuccessful in love, as negative attachment types can be 'healed' by subsequent experience of relationships with securely attached partners.

✔ Arranged marriages may be advisable in cultures where there is little social mobility and few opportunities to meet potential partners. If families did not arrange marriages, it is likely individuals may never meet anyone suitable and compatible.

Western cultures tend to have *voluntary relationships* where individuals have a free choice of partners and may even co-habit before embarking on long-term relationships. Other cultures have *arranged marriages*, where partners are selected by families, with parents having a dominant influence and are more affected by economic considerations than romantic ones. The low divorce rate associated with arranged marriages and evidence suggesting that partners in such relationships develop affection and partner satisfaction over time indicates them to be successful. However, divorce is often harder to obtain in cultures practicing arranged marriages and in such cultures which become more open and display increased rights for women, satisfaction with arranged marriages declines.

Negative evaluation

✘ The continuity hypothesis is opposed by the temperament hypothesis, where the quality of adult relationships is seen as being determined biologically by innate personality. This implies that attempts to improve adult relationships by altering people's attachment styles are doomed to failure.

✘ Much research into cultural influences on romantic relationships is dependent upon self-reports and as such may be highly biased by socially desirable answers where participants answer how their culture would expect them to, rather than give true indications of romantic partner satisfaction.

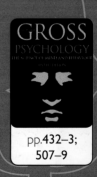

GROSS
PSYCHOLOGY
THE SCIENCE OF MIND AND BEHAVIOUR
6TH EDITION

pp.432–3;
507–9

▲ **Figure 3.4** Bowlby proposed the continuity hypothesis

SOCIAL PSYCHOLOGICAL THEORIES OF AGGRESSION AND INSTITUTIONAL AGGRESSION

Description

Social learning theory (SLT) sees aggression as being learned via observation and imitation of vicariously reinforced aggressive models, where reinforcement is received indirectly by observing other people being rewarded for aggressive behaviour. SLT thus views the acquisition of aggression as occurring through environmental influences rather than innate or internal forces and believes humans are not born aggressive, but acquire it like other social behaviours. *Deindividuation* involves the loss of individual identity and inhibitions when in a crowd, where the capacity for self-awareness and consideration of the consequences of aggressive behaviour is reduced. *Public self-awareness*, where individuals value the impressions they make on others is reduced by the anonymity of crowds, along with a diffusion of responsibility for one's actions,

Additional studies

- Bandura *et al.* (1961, 1963) found that children who had been deliberately frustrated and who saw an adult model behave aggressively to a Bobo doll were likely to imitate specific aggressive acts they had witnessed when allowed to play with the doll and increased aggressive acts if the aggressive model was reinforced. This supports the idea of aggression being learned via SLT.
- Kane & Janus (1981) found that younger and non-white prisoners were more likely to behave aggressively in prison, which suggests that certain groups see themselves as separated from society's values, thus importing their usual aggressive behaviours into prison. This supports the importation model of institutional aggression.
- Cheeseman (2003) reported that prison violence tended to lack any purpose, other than to reduce prisoners' individual levels of stress, demonstrating how the deprivation of liberty and resources leads to stress, which then expresses itself as aggression. This supports the deprivation model of institutional aggression.

while *private self-awareness*, where individuals consider their own thoughts and feelings, is also reduced.

Theories of *institutional aggression* focus on two explanations:

1. The *importation model*, which sees individuals as importing their aggressive tendencies into an institution, such as a prison, and forming an aggressive sub-culture within the institution.

2. The *deprivation model*, which sees aggression as emanating from the injustices and deprivations of institutional life, like the deprivation of liberty within a prison. Such deprivations lead to increased stress, with aggression being used in an attempt to reduce stress and obtain deprived resources and thus gain some control over the social constraints of institutional life.

▲ **Figure 4.1** CCTV cameras make people feel less anonymous and thus less prone to aggression through deindividuation

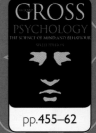

GROSS
PSYCHOLOGY
THE SCIENCE OF MIND AND BEHAVIOUR
SIXTH EDITION

pp.455–62

NEURAL, HORMONAL AND GENETIC FACTORS IN AGGRESSION

Description

Low turnover levels of the neurotransmitter serotonin, where it is recycled slowly after use, are associated with high levels of aggression, while high levels of dopamine have been found to function as a positive reinforcement for aggression, where individuals seek out aggressive situations in order to stimulate their brain-reward system through dopamine release. Testosterone is a male hormone linked to aggression, which is influential soon after birth when testosterone modulates neurotransmitter pathways and in adulthood where sensitisation of neural circuits occurs. Testosterone acts on serotonergic synapses, lowering the amount of serotonin and as low levels of serotonin are associated with aggression, it may be that testosterone modulates the levels of certain neurotransmitters, which mediate effects upon aggression.

Additional studies

- Delville et al. (1997) found that drugs that increased serotonin levels led to a reduction in aggressiveness, which suggests that low levels of serotonin are associated with high levels of aggression. This was supported by Linnoila & Verkunen (1992) finding a correlation between low levels of serotonin and violent behaviour.

- Couppis (2011) placed 'intruder' mice into 'home-based' mice's cages, to which the 'home' mice behaved aggressively. The home mice were then trained to poke a target to get the intruder to return, which they poked continually, indicating that they experienced the aggression as a reward. However, when the home mice had dopamine production suppressed there was a decrease in target poking, which suggests that heightened dopamine functions as a reward for aggressiveness.

- Edwards (1968) found that giving testosterone to neonate female mice made them act aggressively when given testosterone as adults. However, females only given testosterone as adults did not have increased aggressiveness, which suggests that testosterone masculinises androgen-sensitive neural circuits that underpin aggression in the brain.

Positive evaluation

✔ Because research has found that various drugs that reduce serotonic activity increase aggressiveness, certain drugs such as cholesterol-reducing drugs, have been withdrawn from usage.

✔ Much research into neural, hormonal and genetic influences in aggression uses animals, which is beneficial in terms of their faster breeding cycles because it allows cross-generational effects to be seen much more quickly. In addition, much research has been conducted on mice, which is again beneficial as mice have genes and proteins that carry out similar functions in humans.

Research also indicates genetics play a part, as genetics determine testosterone production and its circulatory speed around the body. Genes also establish the synthesis of testosterone receptors and how many and how sensitive such receptors are. Testosterone has been identified as affecting brain function and its contribution to aggression, but genes regulate how much testosterone is produced and how effectively it works. Research also suggests that aggression is influenced by a variation in the MAOA gene that is sensitive to social experiences in early development. This suggests an interaction between genetics and environment in determining aggression, where genes trigger a genetic vulnerability to environmental cues that would explain individual differences in levels of aggression.

Negative evaluation

✘ As research involves animals, there are problems in generalising results to humans, especially as human aggression is more complex and is influenced by mediating factors like cognitive and social factors that are much less so in animals. Another problem with animal studies is that identical brain structures are associated with different types of aggression. The cingulated gyrus is linked to fear-induced aggression in monkeys, but to irritability in cats and dogs.

✘ A genetic basis to aggression is difficult to prove. Many genes seem to be involved, with each variant only having a minute effect on aggressiveness.

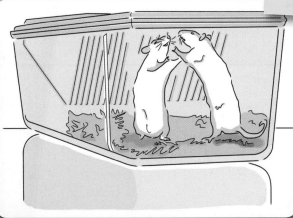

▲ **Figure 4.2** Giving testosterone to neonate female mice makes them aggressive when adult

EVOLUTIONARY EXPLANATIONS INCLUDING INFIDELITY AND JEALOUSY

Focal study

Schutzwohl (2004) gave 200 German participants four scenarios involving social situations, each one with two alternative responses. Only scenario four was of interest and involved imagining one's partner forming an emotional and sexual relationship with someone else. Participants chose whether emotional or sexual involvement made them more jealous and decision times were recorded. Females selecting emotional fidelity reached decisions faster than those choosing sexual infidelity, while males selecting sexual infidelity were quicker to choose than males selecting emotional infidelity. Therefore males and females who select their adaptively primary infidelity type – sexual for men, emotional for women – rely on their initial response tendency suggested by their respective jealousy mechanisms, whereas males and females selecting their adaptively secondary infidelity type engage in additional considerations that override their initial response tendency.

Description

Evolutionary theory views aggression as having a survival value: individuals compete for resources to increase and maintain levels of adaptive fitness, with aggression helping to realise this. Aggressive males had more success competing for reproductive access to females and came to have their genes increasingly represented in the population, so that such aggression became widespread among the species. Females select males on the basis of their resource-richness and thus males evolved the use of aggression as a means of accumulating such resources. Males tend not to aggress against females, as such actions could lessen reproductive opportunities, with the exception of infidelity and jealousy,

Additional studies

- Daly & Wilson (1988) report that a high ratio of murders of partners are conducted by males whose partners have left, or are just about to leave them, due to the jealousy of potentially losing their reproductive capabilities to another male.

- Goetz et al. (2008) found that male aggression against sexual partners was performed in order to punish and deter female infidelity, the intensity and frequency of aggression being related to the degree of suspicion of infidelity. This suggests that such aggressiveness acts as an anti-cuckoldry device in line with evolutionary theory.

- Buunk et al. (1996) found that female jealousy was triggered by a partner displaying interest in other females, which implies an evolutionary female response to potential loss of resources to her and her children. This was supported by Looy (2001) finding that female jealousy occurs through the presence of younger, more attractive women, which again would be a threat to male resource provision.

- Daly et al. (1982) found that men are violent against partners when they are sexually unfaithful, again in line with evolutionary theory.

Positive evaluation

✔ The evolutionary theory of human aggression, including that of jealousy and infidelity, offers a plausible explanation of how such aggression may have arisen through natural selection, especially in terms of gender differences in aggression.

✔ The evolutionary explanation, unlike that of testosterone which mainly focuses on male aggression, is not gender biased, as it encompasses explanations of both male and female aggression as due to different selective pressures.

✔ The evolutionary model of aggression can be used in a practical sense in relationship counselling, especially to help individuals come to terms with why they feel aggressive towards partners due to feelings of jealousy and suspicions of infidelity.

which can result in male aggression against females. Jealousy is a reaction related to a fear of losing access to a reproductive partner and has an element of aggressive anger that serves to maintain sexual associations. Infidelity involves unfaithfulness, with men more at risk of sexual infidelity, as unfaithful females can result in males expending resources on children of uncertain paternity. Females are argued to be more at risk of emotional infidelity, because if males become emotionally involved with non-partners, females risk losing the investment of males' resources in them. Similarly, female jealousy is triggered by the presence of younger and more attractive females who may 'steal' resources and may incur aggression as an attempt to stop this occurring.

▲ **Figure 4.3** Males can act aggressively against female partners if they suspect them of infidelity

Negative evaluation

✘ Studies that show males being more stressed by sexual infidelity may be flawed, as males may actually experience sexual arousal at imagining such scenarios rather than being distressed.

✘ Critics feel that the evolutionary explanation justifies male violence against women as being natural and acceptable.

✘ Evolutionary theory ignores the role of free will in behaviour relating to infidelity and jealousy, seeing aggressive responses as inevitable.

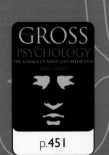

GROSS
PSYCHOLOGY
THE SCIENCE OF MIND AND BEHAVIOUR
SIXTH EDITION

p.451

EVOLUTIONARY EXPLANATIONS OF GROUP DISPLAY

Description

Sport contains actual and ritualised aggression, both of which increase chances of reproductive success. Group displays are ritualised displays of aggression used to determine dominance hierarchies, especially concerning ownership of territory, and also to intimidate others. Group displays are explicable in an evolutionary context, as they help increase status and resource-richness and thus have an adaptive value linked to increased survival. There are several aspects of sport that lend themselves to group displays, both among players and spectators:

● *War dances/supporter displays* concern rituals performed before and during battle to motivate one's own group members and intimidate the enemy. These are amalgamated into sporting contests for the same purposes, for example the *Siva Tau* is a traditional war dance performed by the Samoan rugby team before kick-off.

Additional studies

● Morris (1981) performed a non-participant observation of Oxford United fans, both home and away, finding their behaviour to be extremely territorial and ritualised, which suggests that such group displays have a social purpose explicable in evolutionary terms.

● Sua Peter (2007) reported that in order to reflect the Samoan islanders' warrior past, the Siva Tau, the traditional war dance enacted by Samoan rugby players before a game, was to be revitalised into a more aggressive, intimidatory style, demonstrating the use of group displays in sport.

● End (2005) reported that the environment of sports events are artificially constructed to encourage the use of group displays, which implies that they are social constructions.

● Marsh (1982) found from observations of football fans that most of their aggression was verbal, symbolic, non-serious and relatively harmless and served to reduce levels of actual violence by catharsis — a safe release of negative emotions. This suggests a more psychodynamic than evolutionary explanation.

✓ The similar nature of war dances in different sports and across cultures implies that such behaviours are innate rather than learned, and therefore suggests that such behaviours have an evolutionary origin.

✓ Ritualistic, aggressive group displays in sport may actually be beneficial, as they serve to release aggressive tendencies in a non-harmful way. If group displays were banned, fans may actually resort to real acts of destructive aggression.

✓ Group displays at sports events can actually have a unifying effect where fans from opposite teams are brought together. For example, the common spectacle of the 'Mexican Wave' where fans stand up and sit down in rhythmic unison around the ground.

Other sports use specialist dance troupes, like the Dallas Cowgirls who perform at Dallas Cowboys American football home games, again to rouse the fans and players and to intimidate the opposition. Other supporter displays include wearing replica team shirts, face painting in club colours and singing club anthems.

- *Territorial behaviour* concerns the use of group displays to mark out and defend territories, for example fans using aggression to defend traditional territories and invading the other team's areas.

- *Ritual behaviour* concerns the use of posturing and baiting in a non-violent manner, occurring as a ritualistic display of strength without actual injury to anyone, which again serves to bond and intimidate.

Negative evaluation
✗ Many sports teams' so-called war dances are actually artificial constructions put together and exhibited purely for commercial reasons without any real connection to a warrior past.

✗ Dunning et al. (1998) argued that far from being a ritualistic, harmless display of aggression, much sports-related aggression is truly violent and destructive and can result in serious injuries, including death.

✗ Although group displays can be explained by recourse to evolutionary theory, other factors such as biological, social and cognitive ones should be considered too, in order to have a full understanding of the phenomenon.

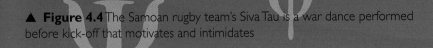

▲ **Figure 4.4** The Samoan rugby team's Siva Tau is a war dance performed before kick-off that motivates and intimidates

FACTORS INFLUENCING ATTITUDES TO FOOD AND EATING AND EXPLANATIONS FOR DIETING SUCCESS OR FAILURE

Focal study

Ogden (2003) tested restraint theory by giving participants either a high-calorie 'pre-load' or a low-calorie snack. After eating, participants were told they were to take a 'taste preference test' and given several foods to taste, the key factor being how much of the taste test food they ate. Of those participants given a high-calorie pre-load, non-dieters reduced their food intake, while dieters ate more. However, dieters given a low-calorie pre-load snack actually ate less during the 'taste preference test'. The findings suggest that although dieters eat less on occasions, restrained eating can also result in over-eating, which explains why many diets fail.

Description

Mood states affect eating behaviour in small ways and in ways incurring large effects, like eating disorders. Mood is affected by stress, which can change an individual's eating habits or eating habits in certain groups.

Cultural influences affect eating behaviour by cultural and sub-cultural groups transmitting different eating practices through operant conditioning and social learning. Some cultural practices result in restricted eating practices, like Jews not eating pork. Culture influences eating behaviour directly, but more often by a moderating effect on variables determining eating practices, like amount of disposable income.

Health concerns affect eating habits, with higher levels of education associated with healthier eating.

Additional studies

1. Wolff *et al.* (2000) reported that female binge eaters had more negative moods on days that they indulged in binge eating than female normal eaters, which suggests that mood does influence eating practices.

2. Stead *et al.* (2004) found that ethnic minority groups lived in poor socio-economic circumstances, had little disposable income and thus ate a poorer diet. They also lacked cooking skills because they were separated from their normal cultural teaching influences, demonstrating how cultural influences can affect eating behaviour.

3. Monneuse *et al.* (1991) found that food items with a lower sugar content were chosen by people with a preference for food with a high sugar content, illustrating that health concerns can affect eating behaviour.

4. Ogden (2003) reported that dieters become increasingly preoccupied with 'forbidden food' items the more they tried to suppress thoughts of such items, which implies that denial creates cognitive stressors that lead to dieting failure.

5. Miller-Kovach *et al.* (2001) reported that over a two-year period diets that included the social support methods of Weight Watchers were more successful than individual diets, illustrating the importance of social support in dieting success.

Positive evaluation

✔ Research into factors influencing eating behaviour has made important contributions to the development of strategies that facilitate successful dieting and help to address the growing problem of obesity.

✔ Cultural eating practices are often shaped to maximise local environmental conditions, such as the seasonal availability of foodstuffs, thus helping members of cultural groupings to eat as healthily as possible in a sustainable manner. Cultural eating practices also help to avoid health risks, for instance it makes sense not to eat meat in cultures where meat can easily become hazardous to health.

Though attitudes may be pro-healthy eating, actual behaviour is moderated by factors like disposable income and the availability of healthy food.

Dieting concerns restrained eating through voluntary restriction of calories. Successful diets set realistic targets and utilise strategies like *relapse prevention,* involving maintaining a stable energy balance around a new lower weight and identifying situations where lapses may occur and creating strategies to refocus when lapses do occur. The use of incentives is important, such as positive reinforcements for achieving weight targets and social support, for example as provided by the organisation Weight Watchers. *Restraint theory* explains failure of dieting as attributable to dieters overeating on occasions, so that overall they eat more than non-dieters. Diets also fail because dieters set unrealistic targets and incur unpleasant side effects of calorie restriction, like giddiness. Dieters also return to old eating habits when targets are reached, resulting in weight gain.

Negative evaluation

✗ Health concerns affect eating practices, but other factors are influential and often override healthy eating intentions. Tuorila & Pangborn (1988) found that the sensory qualities of food affected the consumption of food more than health concerns.

✗ Due to ethical concerns the types of research studies that can be conducted into eating practices and dieting are limited, so self-reports are often used, but incur problems of idealised and socially desirable answers.

▲ **Figure 5.1** Dieters become increasingly pre-occupied with forbidden foods

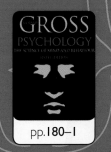

GROSS
PSYCHOLOGY
THE SCIENCE OF MIND AND BEHAVIOUR

pp.180–1

NEURAL MECHANISMS AND EVOLUTIONARY EXPLANATIONS OF FOOD PREFERENCES

Focal study

Hetherington & Ranson (1942) investigated the role of neural structures in the regulation of eating by damaging several brain structures in rats. It was found that large bilateral lesions in the lower central portion of the hypothalamus (the ventromedial nucleus) caused rats to carry on eating until they became grotesquely fat, doubling or trebling their weight. It was concluded that the purpose of the ventromedial hypothalamus is to inhibit feeding when an animal reaches satiety, thus enabling it to maintain a steady energy balance.

Description

The *dual control theory* (DCT) focuses on the idea of a homeostatic control of hunger and satiety, whereby the liver sends signals to the lateral hypothalamus (LH) when glucose levels are low, initiating a sense of hunger to motivate a search for food. The glucose released from the food activates the ventromedial hypothalamus (VMH), initiating a sense of satiety and thus eating stops. DCT was criticised though, as rats were discovered to still be able to reach satiety even if their satiety centre in the VMH was lesioned and still felt hunger if their hunger centre in the LH was lesioned. An alternative to DCT is *set point theory* (SPT), which suggests everyone has an individual metabolic set point – a certain weight their body is geared

Additional studies

- Teitelbaum (1957) trained rats to press a bar to get food and found, in line with DCT, that lesioned VMH rats initially work hard. However, they became less willing to work hard and were fussy eaters, which does not support DCT.

- Powley & Keesey (1970) found that rats who lose weight through starvation and who then have their LH lesioned do not lose further weight, which supports SPT, as it suggests the rats slimmed down to a new set point before the lesions were administered.

- Grill & Norgren (1978) found that neonates display an acceptance of sweet-tasting foods the first time they encounter them, which suggests the preference is innate in line with evolutionary theory.

- Denton (1982) reported that many varying animal species display an innate preference for salt, which suggests the preference has an adaptive value.

- Go et al. (2005) looked at the prevalence of the bitter taste receptor gene T2R in humans and other primates, finding that that humans' bitter-tasting abilities have declined, which suggests that natural selection is acting to reduce human ability to detect bitter tastes.

- Foley & Lee (1991) compared primate feeding strategies with brain size, concluding that meat-eating led directly to increased human intelligence and thus was evolutionarily favoured.

Positive evaluation

✔ SPT is supported by a wealth of research evidence and has been used to create practical applications in the form of therapies to address obesity.

✔ Meat-eating can be dangerous in health terms, but as most cultures have adopted meat-eating, it seems the benefits outweigh the disadvantages, which suggests that a preference for meat has been shaped by evolutionary forces, although greater longevity is associated with vegetarianism.

towards – determined by the rate calories are consumed. An individual's set point can be altered by eating patterns, exercise, etc.

Evolutionary explanations see innate food preferences as having an adaptive advantage linked to survival, such as a preference for sweet-tasting foods, as sweetness indicates a high calorific, non-toxic content. Humans also have a preference for salty foods, as salt is essential for maintaining neural and muscular activity and water balance. Bitter tasting foods are avoided, as bitterness indicates toxicity, humans possessing around 30 genes that code for bitter taste receptors. Humans do not appear to have an innate tendency to eat meat and when and how meat-eating became widespread is debatable, though many see it as linked to the development of intelligence. Meat is rich in energy, but has dangers because of its tendency to become toxic.

Negative evaluation

✘ Although the VMH and LH play an important role in regulating eating behaviour, other factors are involved too, such as biological rhythms. For example, rats begin to eat when darkness falls, a behaviour influenced by the superchiasmatic nucleus, a brain structure in a different part of the hypothalamus.

✘ Although neonate studies imply an innate preference for sweet-tasting foods, interpreting neonates' facial expressions is quite subjective and may be prone to researcher bias.

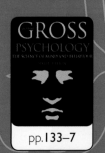

GROSS
PSYCHOLOGY
THE SCIENCE OF MIND AND BEHAVIOUR

pp.133–7

▲ **Figure 5.2** Bitter-tasting foods are avoided as bitterness indicates toxicity

PSYCHOLOGICAL EXPLANATIONS OF OBESITY

Felliti (2001) studied cases of sleep-eating in morbidly obese participants to see if the phenomenon was explicable by psychodynamic means. Five participants with a history of extreme weight fluctuations and sleep-eating were assessed through self-reports on their condition. A common element of sexual abuse in childhood and failed relationships was found, as well as a tendency to lose weight and then put it back on again very quickly through episodes of sleep-eating, of which the participants were unaware. It was concluded that there is a connection between childhood abuse, sleep-eating and obesity. Sleep-eating was interpreted as being an unconscious protective device and anxiety reducer, where eating acts as means of stress reduction and obesity reduces sexual attractiveness.

Description

The *psychodynamic explanation* sees obesity as arising from unresolved childhood conflicts, such as emotional deprivation or over indulgence during the oral stage where the libido is focused on the mouth. During adulthood personality is characterised by oral gratification, which demonstrates itself through overeating. Other factors explicable by psychodynamic means, such as depression and low self-esteem, may also play contributory roles. The psychodynamic explanation is assessed by seeing if psychotherapy reveals underlying childhood traumas and if psychodynamic therapies alleviate the condition.

Behaviourist explanations perceive obesity as caused by maladaptive eating behaviours occurring in three ways:

Additional studies

- Foster (2006) argued that as treatments based on classical conditioning help patients to identify the cues that initiate overeating and to learn new adaptive responses, then the causes of obesity may be due to classical conditioning too.
- Jackson (2008) found that compulsive eating leading to obesity developed from reinforcing good behaviour in children with food, which suggests that operant conditioning in childhood is linked to obesity.
- Hardeman et al. (2000) found that using role models who exhibited healthy eating was an effective means of addressing obesity, which gives support to the social learning explanation of the condition.
- Braet & Crombez (2001) found that obese children were hypersensitive to food-related words, which supports the cognitive explanation by suggesting that an information-processing bias for food stimuli leads to obesity.
- Cserjesi et al. (2007) assessed boys' cognitive profiles to find that obese boys had a deficiency in attention capabilities, which implies that childhood obesity is linked to cognitive deficits.

Positive evaluation

✔ As food is a prime reinforcer and there are many opportunities for using food to reinforce desirable behaviour, it strengthens the idea of operant conditioning being involved with the onset and maintenance of obesity.

✔ Psychological explanations have led to the formation of practical applications in the form of effective therapies to treat obesity. Cognitive behavioural therapy is seen as most effective, with behaviourist treatments proving to be successful too, but as a short-term rather than long-term treatment.

1. *Classical conditioning*, where food cues become associated with the natural pleasure response of food, for example associating eating with watching movies.
2. *Operant conditioning*, where food is used to reinforce desirable behaviours, such as being given food for doing chores.
3. *Social learning theory*, where obesity arises through observation and imitation of obese models. Behaviourist explanations are assessed by seeing if behaviourist therapies effectively treat the condition.

Cognitive explanations see faulty thought processes that underpin maladaptive behaviour as being the cause of obesity. Food and eating become predominate in information processing, as well as a dominant emotional component that sees obese individuals constantly thinking about food and eating. Cognitive explanations are assessed by seeing if faulty thinking does underpin obesity and by whether cognitive therapies are successful in treating obesity.

Negative evaluation

✘ The belief that if a treatment based on an explanation is effective then the explanation must be correct may not be true. The treatment aetiology fallacy argues that it is a mistaken notion to see the success of a treatment as revealing the cause of obesity.

✘ Obesity has reached epidemic proportions and continues to rise. However, there has not been a reported parallel increase in childhood traumas, such as sexual abuse; therefore doubt is cast upon the psychodynamic explanation of obesity.

✘ Cognitive deficits may be an effect rather than a cause of obesity. Elias (2003) reported that early onset obesity leads to a decline in cognitive functioning, weakening support for the cognitive explanation.

▲ **Figure 5.3** Obese children are hypersensitive to food-related words

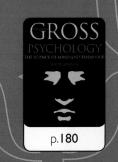

p.180

BIOLOGICAL EXPLANATIONS OF OBESITY

Focal study

Bray et al. (2004) analysed food consumption data from the US Department of Agriculture and found that consumption of *high fructose corn syrup* (HFCS) rose by 1000 per cent between 1970 and 1990 and accounts for 40 per cent of food and drink sweeteners, with each individual American consuming 132kcals of HFCS daily. The rise in HFCS consumption matches the growth in obesity and may be responsible for the rise as it is a foodstuff not familiar to our evolutionary ancestors. HFCS does not stimulate leptin and insulin production, which normally act to regulate eating, suggesting a biological cause to obesity.

Description

The *genetic explanation* of obesity sees the condition as having an innate basis, with some individuals more genetically predisposed to develop obesity than others. The genetic explanation can be combined with the *evolutionary explanation* to explain why only some people become obese.

The evolutionary explanation makes reference to the *thrifty gene model*, where those who carried the gene in the evolutionary past had a selective advantage, as their insulin resistance enabled them to metabolise food more easily. Although this was particularly advantageous in times of food scarcity, it makes them prone to obesity in modern times of food availability.

The *neurological explanation* focuses on the role of the hypothalamus in regulating eating, with obesity seen as due to faulty functioning in the ventromedial hypothalamus, long viewed as the satiety centre, informing individuals when

Additional studies

- Frayling et al. (2007) found that participants with one copy of the fat mass and obesity gene FTO had only a 30 per cent increased risk of becoming obese, while those with two copies of the gene had a 70 per cent increased risk. This supports the genetic explanation and suggests individual vulnerability levels to obesity are genetically determined.
- Rowe et al. (2007) found that Pima Indians have high levels of the thrifty gene and high levels of obesity. The genes allows them to metabolise food efficiently and store excess as fat, useful in an

evolutionary past characterised by periods of food scarcity, but now leading to obesity.

- Reeves & Plum (1969) conducted a post-mortem on an obese female, finding that her VMH was destroyed, which implies the hypothalamus is involved in obesity, suggesting a neurological basis to obesity.
- Kahn & Flier (2000) found that participants who ate large amounts of junk food with a high glycaemic value, contributing to the development of obesity, had high levels of insulin resistance, which suggests that hormonal factors are involved in the onset of the condition.

they are full. Attention has also centred on specific neurological mechanisms, such as the action of the hormone leptin on the POMC and NPY neurones, which through the influence of leptin help regulate appetite.

The *hormonal explanation* links several hormones as having an influence on the development of obesity. Aside from the influence of leptin upon the POMC and NPY neurones, interest has also focused upon three particular hormones:

1. *Insulin*, through its association with the storage and usage of energy, with a link to the genetic explanation, as insulin resistance is genetically influenced.

2. *Cortisol*, through its strong metabolic effect, with high levels of cortisol associated with overeating.

3. *Ghrelin*, through its metabolic slowing effect, whereby individuals have a decreased ability to burn fat.

Positive evaluation

✔ The thrifty gene hypothesis explains why groups of people without the gene can eat a lot and not increase weight, because they live in areas where food shortages did not occur, such as the Nile delta. As a result, the thrifty gene would not have incurred a selective advantage and therefore would not have become more widespread through natural selection.

✔ Practical applications of biological explanations could include genetic profiling to identify individuals most at risk of becoming obese, so that resources could be more effectively targeted.

Negative evaluation

✘ Obesity levels have increased in countries that do not use HFCS, which suggests that the consumption of foodstuffs not present in the evolutionary past cannot explain the rise in global obesity.

✘ Ghrelin antagonists, designed to treat obesity, seem more effective against diabetes, which does not support the idea of ghrelin being a causative factor in developing obesity.

✘ While obesity levels have soared, genes have not changed. However, environmental factors, like the availability of fatty foods, has changed, which implies environmental factors are more important than genetics.

▲ **Figure 5.4** Those without the thrifty gene can consume lots of food without increasing weight

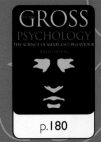

GROSS
PSYCHOLOGY
THE SCIENCE OF MIND AND BEHAVIOUR

p.180

KOHLBERG'S THEORY AND GENDER SCHEMA THEORY

Description

Kohlberg's theory of gender constancy sees children's knowledge of gender roles arising through environmental interactions occurring in three stages:

1. *Gender labelling* (1.5–3 years), where children develop a recognition of their own gender, but understand others' gender purely as labels.

2. *Gender stability* (3–5 years), where children realise that gender is retained for life, but rely on superficial physical signs to determine gender.

3. *Gender constancy* (6–7 years), where children realise that gender is not affected by physical appearance and begin to imitate same-sex models and only indulge in sex-appropriate activities.

Gender schema theory (GST) differs from Kohlberg's theory in seeing no need for children to understand that gender is permanent in order for an understanding of gender to occur. Children

Additional studies

- Emmerlich et al. (1977) found that if children aged 3–5 years encounter someone who is superficially transformed, for example a woman having her hair cut short or a man wearing women's clothes, then they believe the person has changed gender, which supports Kohlberg's stage of gender stability.

- Munroe et al. (1984) reported that the concepts of gender identity, stability and constancy occur in that order of development cross-culturally, which gives Kohlberg's theory added support and suggests that such development has a biological basis.

- Martin & Little (1990) found that gender stereotypes about what is and is not appropriate for boys and girls are held by pre-school children before they develop much understanding of gender, which supports the idea of the formation of gender schemas.

- Martin & Halverson (1983) found that when they asked children to recall pictures of people, children under six years of age recalled more gender-consistent pictures than gender inconsistent pictures, for example they recalled a male footballer rather than a male nurse. This supports the gender schema theory.

are seen as learning appropriate patterns of gender behaviour from observation and imitation and, as with Kohlberg, through active cognitive processing of information that contributes to sex-typing. Once *gender identity* has formed, children start to accumulate knowledge about the sexes into *gender schemas* – organised groups of related concepts. These gender schemas provide a means of interpreting the environment and selecting appropriate types of behaviour, with children's perceptions becoming sex-typed. *In-group schemas* relate to attitudes and expectations relating to one's own gender, while *out-group schemas* relate to the other gender. Toys and games, etc., become categorised as 'for boys' or 'for girls' and children increasingly indulge in gender-stereotyped activities, actively ignoring the other gender.

▲ **Figure 6.1** Children less than six years of age tend to recall more gender-consistent images

Negative evaluation

✘ A major problem for Kohlberg's theory is that it predicts there will be little or no gender-specific behaviour before a child has acquired gender constancy. However, even in infancy girls and boys both display a marked preference for stereotypical male and female toys.

✘ Children adjust their thinking when performing activities not normally stereotypical of their gender, like a girl playing football, so that the activity becomes 'acceptable'. This suggests thinking has been affected by behaviour, but gender schema theory predicts the opposite, thus weakening support for the theory.

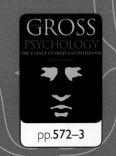

pp.572–3

THE ROLE OF HORMONES AND GENES AND EVOLUTIONARY EXPLANATIONS

Focal study

Deady et al. (2006) assessed the relationship between the importance for females to have children and their levels of testosterone. Twenty-seven women aged 25–30 years completed the Bem Sex Role Inventory, which measures levels of masculinity, femininity and androgyny, with additional questions asked concerning the importance of having children, the ideal number of children, self-rated maternal broodiness and the importance of having a career. Testosterone levels were assessed from saliva samples. Lower testosterone levels correlated with higher scores on the importance of having children and with increased ideal number of children. It was concluded that females' maternal drive is positively related to levels of testosterone.

Description

Biological sex is determined by sex chromosomes: XX for a female and XY for a male. Sex chromosomes contain genetic material that oversees development as a male or female, with sex hormones directing most sexual development. Whether gonads become testes or ovaries is genetically controlled and a surge in testicular hormones makes testosterone levels high in boys, which causes the development of male sex organs and acts on the hypothalamus to masculinise the brain, such as increased ability in spatial awareness. Similarly, the female hormone oestrogen acts to feminise the brain. There are differences in the hypothalamus of males and females, the *sexual dimorphic nucleus* being considerably larger in males with sex hormones believed to be responsible for these differences.

Additional studies

- Hines et al. (2002) found that mothers who had high testosterone levels during pregnancy had healthy daughters who by three and a half years of age demonstrated extremely male-typical toy, playmate and play activity preferences. This suggests that variability in pre-natal androgen levels influences sex-typical play, but without causing gender ambiguity.

- Koopman et al. (1991) found that genetically female mice that lacked the SRY gene developed into male mice when the gene was injected into them, illustrating the important role of genetics in determining gender.

- Wood & Eagly (2002) found that it was characteristic in non-industrialised societies for men to hunt and make tools, while women nurtured children and collected and cooked food. This suggests gender roles are innate and have an evolutionary adaptive advantage.

- Tamares et al. (2002) found that women seek the company of others in times of threat and stress much more than men, which suggests that interpersonal sex roles have been developed through evolutionary forces.

Testes and ovaries help to develop secondary sexual characteristics in puberty.

Evolutionary theory perceives gender roles as occurring due to different selective pressures on males and females, with gender roles being centred on differences in mating strategies. Males are more aggressive in order to compete for reproductive access to females, while females with child-caring duties are nurturing and protective. Cross-cultural research indicates that males and females conduct the gender roles assigned to them by evolution, with males conducting behaviours requiring mobility and power, like hunting, and acquiring greater status as they are free to travel, compete and indulge in trade. Females are restricted to performing activities that can be conducted simultaneously with child caring, such as cooking, farming and gathering fuel.

Negative evaluation

✘ There is little evidence of early behavioural differences between males and females, which would be expected if biological factors were responsible. This suggests that the differences that appear later are due to social factors.

✘ Although research indicates that hormones are involved in gender-related behaviour, such research is correlational and does not indicate causality. Other factors may therefore be involved. For instance, evidence indicates genes are also involved in the masculinisation and feminisation of the brain.

✘ The evolutionary explanation of gender is criticised by some as perceiving gender differences as being biologically inevitable and seeing no influential role for non-biological factors, such as cultural influences.

GROSS
PSYCHOLOGY
THE SCIENCE OF MIND AND BEHAVIOUR
SIXTH EDITION

pp.565–6;
569–70

▲ **Figure 6.2** Cross-cultural studies suggest gender roles are assigned by evolution and possess an adaptive advantage

Focal study

Blanchard et al. (1987) investigated possible differences between homosexual and heterosexual gender dysphorics, as well as prevalence rates between males and females. Seventy-three heterosexual and 52 homosexual gender dysphorics attending a gender identity clinic completed a questionnaire and an interview concerning their condition. It was found that heterosexual males first cross-dressed simultaneously to having cross-gender desires, while homosexual males had cross-gender desires about 3–4 years before cross-dressing. 80 per cent of heterosexual men acknowledged arousal through inanimate objects such as clothing, compared to 10 per cent of homosexual men and 0 per cent of homosexual women. It was concluded that males are not more vulnerable to developing gender dysphoria, but are more susceptible to gender transvestism, being aroused by dressing as a member of the opposite sex.

Description

Biosocial theory sees the interaction of biological and social factors of prime importance, rather than biology's direct influence. From birth the manner in which adults respond to children is influenced by a child's sex, with biosocial theory arguing that it is adults' perception of biological sex that leads to gender identity, as children will be labelled and treated differently according to their sex. Consequently gender is socially constructed, from which gender role identity and sexual orientation emerge, with differences apparent across cultures and over time. Gender role therefore is not set at birth, but is determined as masculine or feminine due to the experiences of growing up, with individuals able to alter and develop in ways not confined by traditional perceptions of male and female behaviour and identity.

Additional studies

- Bradley et al. (1998) reported on a male who had reassignment surgery after damage to his penis and was raised as a girl. The individual preferred female company and, as an adult, happily perceived their self as a female, even though some male behaviour was apparent in childhood. This suggests that biological sex does not determine gender identity.
- Schaffer (2004) found that adults labelled a baby's behaviour and emotions in gender-typical ways according to whether they believed the baby to be male or female, supporting the notion that adults react to gender labels in pre-set ways.
- Hare et al. (2009) found a correlation between gender dysphoria and variants of the androgen receptor gene, which supports the biological explanation, by suggesting the gene is involved in a failure to masculinise the brain during development in the womb.
- Zucker et al. (2008) found that of gender dysphorics aged 2–3 years old referred to a clinic, only 12 per cent of females and 20 per cent of males were still gender dysphoric at age 18, which suggests that gender dysphoria mainly occurs in childhood and is a temporary condition.

Positive evaluation

✔ There are several documented cases of individuals who have received gender reassignment surgery at an early age, who grow up to be happy with their new gender and do not demonstrate gender dysphoria. Such cases therefore support the biosocial approach.

✔ Many gender dysphorics do not perceive their condition as a 'disorder', but instead perceive gender characteristics as a social construction with no relation to biological sex. This suggests that it should be possible for gender dysphorics to alter their gender.

Gender dysphoria is a psychiatric disorder affecting males more than females, which occurs when individuals feel uncomfortable with their biological sex and wish to change it. Research suggests a genetic influence with interest centred on gene variants of the androgen receptor that influence the action of testosterone in masculinisation of the brain, with genetic effects believed to be mediated by hormones. Operant conditioning may also play a role through the attention given to cross-dressing individuals. Early explanations focused on maladaptive learning experiences, maladaptive learning and cognitive experiences and psychodynamic fixations occurring in childhood, but biological explanations have become increasingly favoured and supported.

Negative evaluation

✗ Studies of gender reassignment produce conflicting results and are prone to research bias. Money (1991) reported on 250 cases of individuals being happy with gender reassignment, while Reiner & Gearhart (2003) reported on similar 16 biological males who, after gender reassignment, displayed male characteristics, with 10 deciding to change back to males at age 16.

✗ A downside to gender dysphoria and gender reassignment is that many gender dysphorics suffer social stigmatisation, prejudice and job loss, illustrating the negative consequences of the disorder.

▲ **Figure 6.3** Gender dysphoria occurs when individuals feel uncomfortable with their biological sex

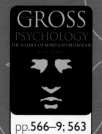

GROSS
PSYCHOLOGY
THE SCIENCE OF MIND AND BEHAVIOUR

pp.566–9; 563

Focal study

Steinke *et al.* (2008) examined gender stereotyping in portrayals of science characters in children's TV programmes. A total of 14 shows with a scientific element were used that were popular with 12–17 year olds. 112 episodes, randomly selected from eight episodes of each programme, were analysed, with 196 scientist characters identified and assessed on gender stereotypical and non-gender stereotypical behaviour. Of these scientist characters, 58 per cent were male and 42 per cent were female, but male scientists were no likelier to be portrayed as high status than females. Though male scientist characters were likelier than females to be portrayed with masculine characteristics of independence and dominance. It was concluded that TV programmes do present gender stereotypes, but that this was becoming less so.

Description

Social learning theory (SLT) sees gender roles as learned via observation and imitation of *socialising agents*. These socialising agents include parents, teachers, peers and the media, who model examples of gender-appropriate behaviour, for which children are reinforced, and examples of gender-inappropriate behaviour, for which children are punished.

Parents are perceived as reinforcing and punishing boys and girls differently according to gender role stereotypes and children may also, by a gradual process of immersion, take on parents' gender schemas.

The *media* is seen as an invasive, persistent social influence on the acquisition, shaping and maintenance of gender roles, by presenting examples of gender-appropriate and inappropriate behaviour, while *peers* exert a social influence

Additional studies

- Huston (1983) found that parents intervene more frequently and quickly in response to aggressive behaviour by girls than boys, illustrating how parents treat children in gender-biased ways.
- Archer & Lloyd (1982) reported that peers ridiculed and ostracised 3-year-olds for playing the opposite sex's games, demonstrating how peers police gender-appropriate behaviour.
- Renzetti & Curran (1992) reported that teachers reinforced girls with praise for being neat, while boys were similarly reinforced for being clever, which supports the notion that teachers enforce gender stereotypes.

- Whiting & Edwards (1988) found that it was cross-culturally universal for girls to be reinforced into domestic and child-nurturing roles, while boys were reinforced into external tasks, like tending animals. This implies that it is the activities children are socialised into that is responsible for differences in gender roles.
- Williams & Best (1990) found there was cross-cultural agreement over which qualities were masculine and feminine. Males tended to be classed as dominant and independent, while females were nurturing and sociable. As children cross-culturally also exhibited these attitudes, it suggests attitudes to gender roles are universal and thus biological in nature.

Positive evaluation

✔ If media sources do exert negative influences in establishing and maintaining traditional gender roles through social learning, then it should be equally possible to establish and maintain positive non-stereotypical gender roles.

✔ Globalisation appears to be leading to a lessening in traditional gender roles cross-culturally, with many cultures seeing increased opportunities for females to indulge in traditionally male-orientated activities and thus attain more power and status within their societies.

through acting as role models and policing gender-appropriate and inappropriate behaviour.

Schools also exert social influences by teachers moderating parental and peer influences, enforcing gender stereotypes and promoting 'girl'- and 'boy'-type subjects.

Cross cultural research allows psychologists to see if gender roles are more innate or learned, though problems occur with cultural bias, the use of culturally inappropriate research methods and tools and researcher bias, such as assuming that males are naturally more aggressive and then only finding examples to confirm this. Some researchers have challenged the western cultural belief that there are only two sexes based on sexual dimorphism, bodily differences between males and females; some cultures acknowledge the existence of up to four separate sexes.

Negative influences

✗ It is difficult to assess how boys learn traditional gender roles by reference to SLT, as Smith & Daglish (1977) found that children are most likely to imitate the parent they have more contact with, which for most children would be the mother.

✗ Attempts to replicate western cultural studies in other cultures can involve an imposed etic, where a situation being studied is assumed to have the same meaning in all cultures. There is also the methodological problem when conducting cross-cultural research of obtaining similar samples and researchers being biased in terms of their own cultural viewpoints.

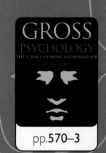

GROSS
PSYCHOLOGY
THE SCIENCE OF MIND AND BEHAVIOUR

pp.570–3

▲ **Figure 6.4** Females are less likely to be presented on TV as scientists

PSYCHOMETRIC AND INFORMATION PROCESSING THEORIES

Focal study

Hunt *et al.* (1973) assessed whether time taken to solve problems correlated with scores of intelligence. Participants were presented with pairs of letters like BB, Bb or Bc and answered as quickly as possible, by pushing a computer button, 'Are the letters the same physically?' or 'Are the letters the same only in name?' The time taken to answer the question about physical similarity was subtracted from the time taken to answer the question on name similarity. A positive correlation was found between speed of retrieval from memory and score on an intelligence test. It was concluded, in line with information processing theories, that intelligence is related to speed of thought.

Description

Psychometric theories believe intelligence is measurable by *factor analysis*, a statistical means of reducing intelligence to its component parts. *Spearman's two-factor model* (1904) argues for two basic factors: a *general intelligence* factor (g), underpinning all intelligent behaviour, which is innate and unaffected by learning, and a *specific factor* (s) relating to particular abilities, like use of vocabulary, which is learned. Spearman saw differences in people's intelligence as being differences in 'g'.

   Guildford's structure of intellect model (1967) argued for 120 separate factors and rejected the notion of 'g'. Guildford saw intelligence consisting of five types of *operation* (type of thinking being performed), four types of *content* (what must be concentrated on) and six types of *product* (type of answer required).

Additional studies

- Johnson & Bouchard (2005), using factor analysis, found a single, higher-order intelligence factor, which supports the idea of a general intelligence factor underpinning intelligence, in line with Spearman's theory.
- Guildford (1985) found that the scores achieved on tests he had devised to measure separate mental abilities often correlated with each other, which implies that there are probably fewer than the 120 separate mental abilities he had originally claimed existed.
- Merrick (1992) applied factor analysis to data gained on cognitive abilities from Dutch high school girls, finding individuals with all three types of intelligence suggested by Sternberg, thus supporting the existence of these components.
- Marchand (2008) found that mud masons in Mali communicated building skills without formal teaching using verbal instruction, but instead by physical repetition, supporting Gardner's notion of a bodily kinaesthetic intelligence and thus the idea of multiple intelligences.
- Turner (2008) reported that teachers successfully used memorable tunes to fit in lyrics relating to subject matter being taught and that students with advanced levels of musical intelligence recalled more of the content, providing further support for Gardner's theory.

Information processing theories focus on the cognitive processes used to solve problems. *Steinberg's triarchic theory* (1977) believed psychometric theories only measured 'school smartness' and neglected 'street smartness'. Steinberg's theory has three facets:
1. *analytical intelligence*, involving *metacomponents, performance components* and *knowledge acquisition components*
2. *creative intelligence*, involving *novelty* and *automation*
3. *practical intelligence*, involving *adaptation, shaping* and *selection.*
Gardner's theory of multiple intelligences (1983) sees individuals possessing a *cognitive profile* of differing amounts of various types of intelligence: *bodily kinaesthetic* (concerning bodily movements), *interpersonal* (concerning interactions with others), *intrapersonal* (concerning self-awareness), *linguistic* (concerning the use of language), *logical-mathematical* (concerning logic), *musical* (concerning sensitivity to sound), *spatial* (concerning visual and spatial judgement) and *naturalistic* (concerning the natural world).

Positive evaluation

✔ Spearman's theory was groundbreaking, as it stimulated interest and became the theoretical foundation upon which many similar theories were based.

✔ Guildford's theory was used to create the **structure of intellect** (SOI) teaching programme, which creates individual profiles based on identification of strengths and weaknesses. SOI has proved effective in helping gifted children to think more creatively.

✔ Sternberg's theory has a broader scope in assessing synthetic and practical skills, as well as analytical skills and thus is more inclusive by accounting for both 'school smart' and 'street smart' children.

Negative evaluation

✘ Because factor analysis produces a wide range of basic factors, from Spearman's two factors to Guildford's 120, it suggests the technique is not as objective and scientific as claimed.

✘ Gardner's intelligence types may simply be aspects of personality rather than types of intelligence, especially as there are no tests to identify and measure them.

✘ Gottfredson (2003) criticised Sternberg's theory for being non-scientific, claiming Sternberg's practical intelligence is not a form of intelligence, but merely task-specific knowledge relatable to specific environments.

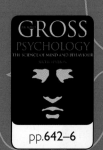

pp.642–6

▲ **Figure 7.1** Mud masons in Mali learn from physical repetition, which relates to Gardner's idea of bodily kinaesthetic intelligence

SIMPLE LEARNING IN ANIMALS AND INTELLIGENCE IN NON-HUMAN ANIMALS

Description

Simple learning concerns *classical conditioning*, involving association of neutral stimuli with involuntary unconditioned stimuli and operant conditioning, involving reinforcement of behaviour to increase chances of the behaviour recurring. *Positive reinforcement* occurs where something pleasant is received for exhibiting a behaviour, while *negative reinforcement* occurs by not receiving something unpleasant for exhibiting a behaviour. Animals use simple learning to learn about their environment and to adapt to changing environments. Seligman (1970) proposed *biological preparedness*, where some associations are easily learned, as animals are more biologically predisposed to do so.

Intelligence in non-human animals is linked to survival and occurs as a hierarchy of learning processes, with species differing in the amount of their behaviour that is learned. *Social learning*

Additional studies

- Garcia et al. (1990) found that wolves and coyotes made ill by eating mutton laced with lithium chloride would not approach sheep, instead showing submissive behaviour to them, which demonstrates classical conditioning at work in the real world.
- Wehner et al. (1996) reported how ants learn to use landmarks through trial and error learning when navigating a familiar area, illustrating the use of operant conditioning in real-life settings.
- Tomasello et al. (1987) reported how chimpanzees did not imitate the specific actions of a model, but developed personal techniques when using a rake to obtain food,

suggesting that emulation was occurring, where the consequences of an action rather than the actual action are reproduced.

- Cheney & Seyfarth (1988) found that Vervet monkeys learned to ignore a particular monkey's 'leopard alarm call' when it was played continually and there was no leopard around, but still reacted to other monkeys' alarm calls. This suggests that Vervet monkeys have a ToM.
- Nishida et al. (1992) found that alpha males do not share food with close rivals, but would share with non-rivals; so that they would assist the alpha male in future power struggles, demonstrating the use of Machiavellian intelligence.

refers to social interactions that affect what animals learn. With *imitation* behaviour is observed and copied, while with *enhancement* attention is directed to particular features of the environment in order to solve problems.

Emulation involves reproduction of the consequences of behaviour, rather than direct imitation, and *tutoring* involves animals acting as models to others, at a price to the model.

Self-recognition is a form of intelligence involving self-awareness, for instance being able to recognise one's own image in a mirror, while *theory of mind* (ToM) is the idea that some species can attribute mental states, like beliefs and intents, onto themselves and others, which assists in explaining and predicting others' behaviour.

Machiavellian intelligence concerns serving personal interests by manipulation of or cooperation with others, without upsetting the social cohesion of a group.

▲ **Figure 7.2** Ants learn to navigate using landmarks through operant conditioning

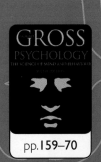

GROSS
PSYCHOLOGY
THE SCIENCE OF MIND AND BEHAVIOUR

pp.159–70

EVOLUTIONARY FACTORS IN HUMAN INTELLIGENCE

Description

Evolutionary theory sees human intelligence as having evolved due the demands of an ever-changing environment creating selective pressure for an advanced intellect. Humans developed intelligence in order to meet *ecological demands* (features of the environment providing a survival value). An example of this is the development of foraging abilities, like monitoring the seasonal availability of foodstuffs, finding hidden foods like roots and creating tools to exploit them. The *social complexity hypothesis* (SCH) perceives high levels of intelligence as advantageous to animals living in complex social groups. SCH proposes that animals living in large complex groups should exhibit advanced cognition skills.

Additional studies

- Milton (1988) reported that fruit-eating spiders have greater relative brain size, bigger home territories and a lengthier learning/dependency period, supporting the idea of greater intelligence evolving in fruit-eating spiders in order to meet ecological demands.
- Holekamp & Engh (2003 and 2004) studied spotted hyenas and other social carnivores to find a positive correlation between size of brain structures and complexity of social living. From data relating to who group members formed alliances with, it was found that hyenas calculated other group members' status, suggesting that intellectual abilities are shaped by the environmental demands of social living in line with SCH.
- Lynn (1989) used fossil evidence to report that during the evolution of humans, brain size increased by 300 per cent, which suggests that having larger brains incurs an adaptive advantage in line with evolutionary theory.
- Byrne (1995) reported that neocortical brain enlargement correlates more with social group size and the complexity of social relationships, which suggests that greater intelligence developed more in social animals adding further support to evolutionary explanations of human intelligence.

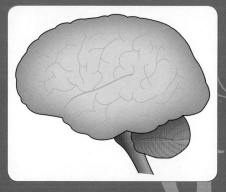

▲ **Figure 7.3** The human brain consumes 35 per cent of calorific intake

Brain size is also important, with larger brains having evolved to meet the demands of social living, like Machiavellian intelligence, ecological demands and other environmental pressures. Also of importance is *transitive inference* where observation of events on a repeated basis leads to individuals being able to deduce the probability of that and other events occurring. Large brains have a cost though: giving birth to a large-headed baby is problematic and an intelligent brain needs a lot of energy – human brains consume 35 per cent of calorific intake. The fact that large brains have evolved suggests that the adaptive advantages of a larger brain outweigh the disadvantages.

Positive evaluation

✔ Different foraging skills use different brain areas: the neocortex for monitoring and extracting foodstuffs and the hippocampus, prefrontal and parietal lobes for the construction of mental maps, illustrating the complex relationship between evolution and human intelligence.

✔ Research indicates that neocortical brain growth is positively correlated with group size, lending support to the SCH.

✔ The fact that crows – birds with small brains – demonstrate intelligent tool use contradicts evolutionary explanations. However, crows do have a relatively large cortex, which is associated with higher intelligence in line with evolutionary theory.

Negative evaluation

✘ The development of tools to extract foodstuffs may be an effect of intelligence rather than a cause, as animals extracting only one foodstuff use tools in a less intelligent way, while those extracting many foodstuffs show more intelligent tool use.

✘ Assessing animal studies, like those involving transitive inference, involves subjective interpretation and thus may be prone to researcher bias.

✘ Forty per cent of children with abnormally small brains are not retarded in intelligence, which implies that brain size is not linked to intelligence, lessening support for evolutionary explanations.

Focal study

Heber et al. (1972) assessed whether deprived children's IQ was boosted by environmental enrichment. Twenty black mothers of IQ below 80, with newborn disadvantaged children, were given education, job training, homemaking and childcare tuition, while their children received regular enrichment. Twenty similar mothers and children received no enrichment. At age 6 the enriched children had average IQ of 121 compared to the non-enriched children's 87. By age 10 the enriched children's average IQ fell to 105 compared to the non-enriched children's 85. Therefore enrichment boosts IQ, but only while enrichment continues.

Description

IQ tests assume that general intelligence exists, is innate, is unaffected by environmental influences and is measureable. Opponents claim they measure educational attainment, not natural talent. Various research methods are used to evaluate the relative contributions of genetics and environment, though most psychologists believe both heredity and environment contribute to intelligence and interact in various ways. Twin studies compare the IQ levels of monozygotic twins (MZ), who share 100 per cent of their genes, and dizygotic twins (DZ), who share 50 per cent of their genes. Studies indicate that the closer people's genetic similarity, the closer their IQ levels, but as genetic similarity increases so does environmental similarity. The solution to this is to study separated identical twins, with again heredity seeming to be favoured, but

Additional studies

- Bouchard & McGue (1981) found IQ correlations of 86 per cent for MZ twins reared together, 72 per cent for those reared apart and 60 per cent for DZ twins reared together, which suggests that intelligence is predominantly genetic in origin.

- Capron & Duyme (1989) found that children adopted before six months of age by adoptive parents of high socio-economic status had higher IQs than similar children raised by parents of low socio-economic status, illustrating the significance of environment in determining intelligence.

- Lahn et al. (2004) identified a link between the ASPM gene and higher intelligence. ASPM affects the expansion of the cerebral cortex, supplying a possible explanation of how genes affect intelligence.

- Saltz (1973) found that children in institutional care, paired with foster grandparents who provided social stimulation for four years, outscored in IQ similar children not receiving such enrichment. This suggests environmental enrichment can boost intelligence.

- Mortenson et al. (2002) found a positive correlation between duration of breastfeeding and IQ scores, which suggests nutrition during early development is influential in determining intelligence.

- Williams (1972) found that black people outscored white people on an IQ test based on black culture, illustrating the cultural nature of intelligence.

Positive evaluation

✔ The benefits of enrichment programmes are not limited to boosting IQ levels; there are other advantages too, like the elevation of motivational and confidence levels, which contribute to heightened school attainment and the benefits that brings.

✔ The diathesis-stress model explains how genes and environment interact in realising IQ levels. Individuals have genetically pre-determined IQ potentials, with the quality of environment determining how much potential is realised.

there are criticisms as to how separated such twins are. Adoption studies compare the IQ levels of adopted children with their adoptive parents, with whom they share little genetic similarity, but much environmental similarity, against that of their biological parents, with whom they share no environmental similarity, but much genetic similarity. It is also possible to see if IQ levels move away from or towards those of adoptive families. Technological advances have seen the development of gene mapping studies, which have identified several genes associated with the heritability of intelligence. Research also examines several environmental influences, like enrichment programmes that seek to boost IQ and the effect of diet on IQ. Intelligence is also seen to be culturally based, meaning that IQ tests, based on western cultural viewpoints, are not applicable in all cultures.

Negative evaluation

✗ 'Separated' MZ twins often have similar backgrounds, like being raised by similar families. Shields (1962) found an IQ correlation of only 51 per cent in MZ twins raised in dissimilar families, thus casting doubt on the hereditary argument.

✗ Enrichment programmes are difficult to evaluate, as they often differ widely in how they are applied in different locations and individual circumstances. They are also affected by bias in terms of political and philosophical viewpoints concerning the nature of intelligence; researchers who believe intelligence is genetic tend to interpret findings to that end and vice versa.

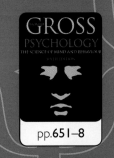

pp.651–8

▲ **Figure 7.4** Black people outscore white people on IQ tests based on black culture

57

PIAGET AND VYGOTSKY'S THEORIES AND THEIR APPLICATION TO EDUCATION

Focal study

Piaget & Inhelder (1956) assessed whether children below 7 years were egocentric (i.e. only see the world from their viewpoint). Participants aged 4–8 years explored a model of three mountains of different colours and toppings and then sat on one side of the model opposite a doll. Participants had to select from 10 different pictures, which represented the doll's view. It was found that 4-year-olds chose the picture representing their own view; 6-year-olds displayed some awareness of others' views, but generally chose the wrong picture, while 7- and 8-year-olds consistently chose the picture representing the doll's view. It was concluded that children under 7 are generally egocentric.

Description

Piaget believed that infants are born with innate *schema* (ways of understanding the world). If new experiences fit existing schema they are *assimilated*, if not *disequilibrium* occurs (a state of mental unbalance) with individuals motivated to return to *equilibrium* (a state of mental balance) by *accommodation* (altering schema to fit in new experiences). Assimilation and accommodation form the invariant process of *adaptation*, with equilibrium and disequilibrium forming the invariant process of *equilibration*. Schemas and *operations* (strings of schemas assembled in logical order) are variant structures that change as individuals develop through a series of fixed stages: *sensorimotor* (0–2 years), *pre-operational* (2–7 years), *concrete operational* (7–11 years) and *formal operational* (11+ years). Vygotsky saw cognitive development as a cultural concept, with cognitive development involving

Additional studies

- Piaget (1952) found that 7-year-olds could not conserve liquid, believing that when one of two identical beakers of water was poured into an equal, but taller and thinner beaker, it contained more water than the original. This supports the idea that children of that age are in the pre-operational stage, where children are influenced by how things seem.

- Wood et al. (1976) found that 4–5-year-olds fitting blocks into a pyramid learned best with 'sensitive guidance' where children were given assistance when they got stuck by mothers acting as tutors. Verbal instructions that were difficult to understand were ineffective, as was a full demonstration of the solution. This supports Vygotsky's idea of the ZPD.

- Danner & Day (1977) found that coaching 10–13-year-olds had no effect, supporting Piaget's concept of readiness, though it did assist 17-year-olds, which implies that tuition assists at later stages of development.

- Bennett & Dunne (1991) found that more logical thinking, less competitiveness and interest in status was demonstrated by children working in cooperative groups, giving support to Vygotsky's concept of collaborative thinking.

an active internalisation of problem-solving processes occurring through mutual interaction between children and those they socially interact with. *Scaffolding* (tuition given by more knowledgeable others) permits children to independently perform tasks, occurring within the *zone of proximal development* (ZPD) (the distance between current and potential ability).

Piaget's theory relates to education through: *the concept of readiness*, where children's learning is constrained by their stage of development, *discovery learning*, which emphasises child-centred learning and *the curriculum*, where certain things are taught at certain ages. Vygotsky's theory relates to education through *collaborative learning*, where children of similar competence work together, *peer tutoring* to create meaningful learning experiences and *scaffolding*, where children are given clues rather than facts.

Positive evaluation

✔ Piaget's theory stimulated much interest and research into cognitive development that led to the formation of other related theories that addressed the shortcomings of Piaget's theory, such as Bruner's modes of representation.

✔ Vygotsky's theory explains (which Piaget's theory does not) the influence of the social environment through culture and language upon cognitive development.

✔ Piaget's theory influenced education. The Plowden report (1967) led to primary education moving from being teacher-led to child-centred.

Negative evaluation

✗ Vygotsky's theory overemphasises the influence of social factors at the expense of individual and biological factors. If development depended solely on social factors learning would occur faster.

✗ Dasen (1977) argued that as formal operational thinking is not found in all cultures, then this particular stage is not under genetic control. Even in cultures where it is found, not all individuals acquire it.

✗ Some children learn best alone, not through collaborative thinking, which suggests Vygotsky's teaching methods are not applicable to all.

✗ Piaget's research was conducted on children of well-educated professionals; therefore the findings are not necessarily generalisable to everyone.

▲ **Figure 8.1** Piaget's theory stimulated much interest and research into cognitive development

GROSS
PSYCHOLOGY
THE SCIENCE OF MIND AND BEHAVIOUR

pp.528–35;
550–2;
539–42

KOHLBERG'S THEORY OF MORALITY

Focal study

Kohlberg (1958) investigated the moral reasoning of children and adolescents. Seventy-two boys aged 10, 13 and 16 were individually interviewed by being given ten moral dilemmas to assess their level of moral reasoning, in which accompanying questions were asked illustrating that in real-life there is no single 'right' answer. Each interview lasted two hours. For each dilemma which stage of moral reasoning that best fitted an individual's answer was decided. The children were assessed for 26 more years. Children aged 10 generally displayed stage 2 reasoning, with examples of stages 1 and 3. By age 22 stages 3 and 4 predominated and by age 36 only 5 per cent had reached stage 5, with stage 6 only rarely attained. It was concluded that morality progresses with age.

Description

Kohlberg's theory is based on cognitive development, perceiving morality as developing gradually in a number of innate stages, in a set order, during childhood and adolescence. Morality develops with biological maturation and when experiences go against current schemas to challenge current thinking about morality. His interest was in people's reasoning in reaching moral judgements rather than the judgements themselves, for example, people's reasons for upholding the law and whether they thought there were circumstances in which breaking the law was justifiable. Kohlberg assessed moral reasoning through the use of *moral dilemmas*, involving a choice between two alternatives, both of which were socially unacceptable, for instance whether it was right to break the law and steal a drug that could save a loved one's life. He saw

Additional studies

- Rest (1983) performed a 20-year longitudinal study of males from adolescence to their mid-30s that showed development through the stages, occurring in the order described by Kohlberg, giving support to his theory.
- Berkowitz & Gibbs (1983) found that discussions about moral possibilities quickened development through the stages, which suggests that creating disequilibrium in an individual's moral thinking develops moral progression, though only when biological maturation permits, in line with Kohlberg's theory.

- Walker et al. (1987) found evidence to support Kohlberg, in that children of age 10 exhibit stage 2 moral reasoning, while children of age 16 had progressed to stage 3. However, they proposed that there were nine stages to explain the finding that children's moral reasoning often sits between stages.
- Fodor (1972) found that non-delinquent children's levels of morality were higher than delinquent children's, which implies that moral reasoning does actually underpin moral behaviour, as proposed by Kohlberg.

women as less morally developed due to females being constrained by domesticity. Kohlberg proposed that there were three levels of morality, each containing two stages, all different, as they involve different types of moral thinking:

● *Pre-conventional morality* (6–13 years) – stage one, morality based on avoiding punishment; stage two, moral rules are followed when it suits us.

● *Conventional morality* (13–16 years) – stage three, morality based on pleasing and helping others; stage four, morality based on maintaining social order.

● *Post-conventional morality* (16–20 years) – stage five, laws are breakable if destructive; stage six, morality based on personal moral rules.

▲ **Figure 8.2** Gilligan examined the moral reasoning behind the real-life scenario of deciding whether or not to have an abortion

Negative evaluation

✘ Children do not understand the moral reasoning illustrated in Kohlberg's dilemmas, highlighting some methodological flaws in his research. Children do, however, have experience of moral reasoning through everyday occurrences like sharing food and toys, which could form the basis for more appropriate dilemmas.

✘ Moral dilemmas do not possess the emotional impact of real-life scenarios and thus participants may have behaved differently if actually placed in those situations. Gilligan (1982) examined the moral reasoning of females deciding whether to have abortions, finding a different pattern of moral reasoning to Kohlberg.

✘ Kohlberg's view of female morality was impoverished. While male morality is based on abstract principles of law and justice, female morality is based on principles of care and compassion.

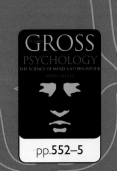

GROSS PSYCHOLOGY
THE SCIENCE OF MIND AND BEHAVIOUR
pp.552–5

DEVELOPMENT OF THE CHILD'S SENSE OF SELF AND UNDERSTANDING OF OTHERS

Description

Part of developing a sense of 'self' is the ability to self-recognise. Self-recognition is tested with the *mirror test*, where a coloured facial mark is made and participants placed in front of a mirror to see if they touch the mark. If an infant understands the image is them, then it has a mental representation of itself. Some do this by 15 months and most by two years of age. Also important is Theory of Mind (ToM), concerning the ability to attribute mental states, knowledge, wishes, feelings and beliefs to oneself and others. ToM is tested with *false belief tasks*, where participants witness an event and then while a person is absent the scene is altered. The idea is to see if participants describe the scene as known to them or to the returning person, i.e. can they picture the scene through another's eyes. ToM is

Additional studies

- Mans *et al.* (1978) reported that self-recognition in Down's syndrome children does occur, but is delayed until four years of age when 89 per cent could pass the mirror test. As cognitive development occurs more slowly in Down's syndrome children, it suggests that self-recognition and thus self-awareness is related to cognitive development.

- Wimmer & Perner (1983) found that most 6- and 8-year-olds correctly realised that a model doll would look for a hidden chocolate where he had seen it stored and not where they themselves had seen it moved to. As most 4-year-olds could not do this, it implies ToM develops at 6–8 years.

- Bartsch & Wellman (1995) found that there is a common developmental pattern in the acquisition of ToM in American and Chinese children, suggesting the ability to be under genetic control.

- Schultz & Selman (1990) reported that the development from self-centred perspectives to being able to see from others' perspectives is related to the development of heightened interpersonal negotiation skills and concern for others, which implies that perspective taking helps to achieve social maturity.

not acquired until cognitive development is sufficient, at around four years of age. With the development of ToM comes the ability to manipulate and deceive by hiding one's emotions and intentions.

Perspective taking involves the ability to assume other people's viewpoints and understand their thoughts and feelings. Selman (1980) devised *role-taking theory* to explain the development of perspective taking, which has five stages:
1. Stage 0 – *egocentric viewpoint* (3–6 years)
2. Stage 1 – *social informational role taking* (6–8 years)
3. Stage 2 – *self-reflective role taking* (8–10 years)
4. Stage 3 – *mutual role taking* (10–12 years)
5. Stage 4 – *social and conventional system role taking* (12–15+).

▲ **Figure 8.3** The mirror test is the standard means of assessing self-recognition

GROSS
PSYCHOLOGY
THE SCIENCE OF MIND AND BEHAVIOUR
sixth edition

pp.519–25; 534

BIOLOGICAL EXPLANATIONS OF SOCIAL COGNITION

Focal study

Dapretto et al. (2006) compared motor neuron ability in autistic and normal children. A sample of ten high-functioning autistic children and ten normally functioning children were presented with 80 faces, representing emotions of anger, fear, sadness, happiness and neutrality for two seconds each in a random sequence. fMRI (functional magnetic resonance imaging) scans were performed as participants either observed or imitated the faces presented. The degree of mirror neuron activity and symptom severity was also assessed in the autistic children. It was found that both groups observed and imitated the faces, but autistic children had no mirror neuron activity in the inferior frontal gyrus (pars opercularis) brain area. A negative correlation occurred between activity in the pars opercularis, insula and limbic structures and severity of autism symptoms. It was concluded that mirror neurons underlie the ability to read other's emotional states from facial expressions.

Description

Humans are sociable animals and their ability to be socially interactive relies upon developing brain systems focused on processing social information. Learning experiences are required for normal development of such abilities, but only by reference to innate neural systems can the universality and speed of development of social cognition be understood. *Mirror neurons* are nerves in the brain, active when specific actions are performed or viewed in others, permitting observers to experience those actions as if their own. Mirror neurons therefore allow humans to share in the emotions and cognitions of others by empathy with and imitation of others. They also permit us to have

Additional studies

- Rizzalato & Craighero (2004) found that the same mirror neurons fire when monkeys perform and observe specific motor acts, such as picking up a peanut, demonstrating that there is a neural basis to actions being represented in a form that applies to performing and observing actions.

- Blakemore et al. (2005) found that touching the face and neck and watching others being touched activated the primary and secondary somatosensory cortex – brain areas associated with the sense of touch. As this occurs unconsciously, it suggests mirroring others' emotions and experiences is an automatic process.

- Wicker et al. (2003) found that the inferior frontal cortex and anterior cingulate cortex are activated when smelling an unpleasant odour and by observing the facial disgust of others smelling the odour. This implies that mirror neuron activity permits empathy with others' emotions.

- Stuss et al. (2001) found that individuals who could not empathise easily with others, read their intentions and were easily deceived, had damaged frontal lobes, which suggests that abnormalities in social cognition have a biological basis.

Positive evaluation

✔ The fact that social cognition skills are found only in higher animals that live in complex social groupings suggests that such abilities have an evolved adaptive value and thus a biological basis to them.

✔ The development of positron emission tomography (PET) and fMRI brain-scanning techniques have allowed psychologists to perform research into social cognition that has greatly contributed to an understanding of the phenomenon.

✔ The exploration of the neural basis to social behaviour suggests that certain brain structures are specialised for social interactions and allow humans to engage in meaningful interactions.

a ToM. Brain imaging studies show that when an individual experiences an emotion, such as pleasure, and witnesses a facial expression of pleasure in another individual, the same motor neurons are activated. Therefore individuals can have direct experiential comprehension of each others' feelings, thoughts and actions, which explains how people empathise with each other. Research indicates that mirror neurons are located in brain areas dealing with social cognition, especially motor-related areas. Mirror neurons may allow psychologists to understand others' mental states, with defective mirror neuron systems providing the key to explaining abnormalities in social communication and interaction, such as autism.

▲ **Figure 8.4** The same mirror neurons fire when monkeys observe and perform the same actions

Negative evaluation

✗ A methodological problem in studying mirror neuron activity in humans is not being able to study the actions of single neurons.

✗ An explanation of social cognition based on mirror neurons is oversimplistic, as it cannot explain how actions performed by others can be interpreted differently by someone observing in different contexts.

✗ Much research into the actions of mirror neurons has been done on animals, such as with monkeys, and therefore presents problems of generalisation to humans.

SCHIZOPHRENIA

Description

Schizophrenia affects thought processes and the ability to determine reality. *Type I* is characterised by positive symptoms, with better prognosis for recovery. *Type II* is characterised by negative symptoms, with poorer prognosis for recovery. *First rank symptoms* are mainly positive ones: passivity experiences and thought disorders, auditory hallucinations and primary delusions. *Additional symptoms* are mainly negative ones: thought process disorders, disturbances of effect, psychomotor disturbances and lack of volition.

Classification systems, such as DSM (Diagnostic and Statistical Manual of Mental Disorders) and ICD (International Classification of Diseases), have become increasingly reliable and valid over time.

With *biological explanations*, research involving twin and adoption studies suggests *genetics* determine levels of vulnerability, while the *biochemical explanation* perceives an excess of dopamine as being linked to schizophrenia.

Additional studies

- Hollis (2000) found a high level of stability to diagnoses of schizophrenia based on DSM classification systems, which suggests diagnosis is mainly valid.
- Kety & Ingraham (1992) found that adoptive schizophrenics' genetic relatives had a prevalence level of schizophrenia ten times that of their adopted relatives, which implies that genes play a larger role than environment.
- Iversen (1979) found excess dopamine in the limbic systems of dead schizophrenics, supporting the biochemical explanation.
- Fisk (1997) found ECT had a success rate of 60–80 per cent, but is effective only against certain types of schizophrenia and needs more treatments than with other disorders, implying ECT to be only partially effective.
- Malmberg & Fenton (2009) found psychodynamic therapies have little benefit unless combined with drug treatment, suggesting the treatment is effective as a combination therapy.
- Tarrier (2005) found that research studies provided persistent evidence that CBT incurred reduced symptoms, especially positive ones, produced lower relapse rates and a speedier recovery in acute cases. This indicates the treatment to be highly effective.

Positive evaluation

Positive evaluation

✔ The DSM classification system is more reliable than the ICD, because there is more specificity of symptoms outlined in each category.

✔ Evidence from genetic studies support the diathesis-stress model, which sees individuals inheriting a genetic vulnerability and then environmental triggers determining if the condition is developed.

✔ Antipsychotics are relatively cheap to manufacture, easy and familiar to take and allow countless schizophrenics to live relatively normal lives. They also incur big financial savings in keeping sufferers outside of institutional care.

✔ Considerable evidence suggests CBT to be the most effective psychological treatment.

With *psychological explanations*, research suggests that maladaptive thinking is linked to many schizophrenic symptoms, suggesting a *cognitive explanation*, while *socio-cultural explanations* focus on social and cultural factors, like the family and social environments.

Biological therapies mainly centre on *antipsychotic drugs* that enable many schizophrenics to live relatively normal lives outside of institutions. First generation antipsychotics arrest dopamine production to reduce positive symptoms, while second generation antipsychotics act on serotonin and dopamine systems. Both incur side effects. *Electro-convulsive therapy* (ECT), reintroduced to treat schizophrenia, is more effective than no treatment, but is not as effective as drugs.

Psychological therapies occur in several forms, like *psychodynamic therapy*, which attempts to provide insight into the link between symptoms and early experiences that lead to faulty metarepresentation of thinking. *Cognitive behavioural therapy* (CBT) attempts to modify hallucinations and delusional beliefs by illuminating the links between sufferers' thoughts, actions and emotions.

▲ **Figure 9.1** Anti-psychotics are cheap, easy and familiar to take and allow many schizophrenics to live relatively normal lives

Negative evaluation

✗ Excess dopamine may be an effect of rather than a cause of schizophrenia, weakening support for the biochemical explanation. Similarly, socio-cultural factors may be effects rather than causes of schizophrenia; expressed emotions, like hostility, may occur due to the stresses of living with a schizophrenic rather than contributing to its onset.

✗ Of schizophrenics receiving ECT, 20–50 per cent relapse within six months, suggesting the treatment is not effective in the long term.

✗ Evidence suggests that psychodynamic therapies are more harmful than helpful. Stone (1986) reported a high suicide rate among those receiving such treatments.

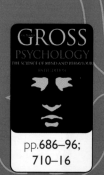
GROSS PSYCHOLOGY
pp.686–96; 710–16

DEPRESSION

Description

Depression is a mood disorder characterised by extended and deep disturbance of emotions. *Unipolar depression* involves just depression, while *bipolar depression* involves episodes of depression and mania. Depression is also seen as *endogenous*, related to internal biochemical and hormonal factors, and *exogenous*, related to external factors like stress.

The clinical characteristics of depression are constant depressed mood, lessened interest, weight loss, sleep pattern disturbance, fatigue, reduced concentration, worthlessness and focus on death. As moods vary, reliability and validity of diagnosis can be problematic.

Biological explanations include *genetics*, where studies indicate a genetic vulnerability to depression and *biochemical explanations*, where abnormal levels of hormones and neurotransmitters are perceived as causing depression.

Additional studies

- Van Weel-Baumgarten (2000) found that Dutch doctors using DSM-IV criteria correctly diagnosed 28 out of 33 depressed patients, which suggests validity of diagnosis is fairly high.
- Mann *et al.* (1996) found that serotonin deficiency and insufficient serotonin receptors resulted in unipolar depression, supporting the idea of a biochemical explanation.
- Coleman (1986) found that individuals who received low amounts of positive reinforcement for social behaviours became increasingly non-responsive socially, resulting in depression, which implies a behaviourist cause.
- Boury *et al.* (2001) found that depressive individuals foresee the future negatively and misinterpret facts and experiences negatively, supporting the cognitive explanation.
- Furukawa *et al.* (2003) found from a review of 35 studies that placebos were inferior to antidepressants, illustrating the effectiveness of drug treatments in addressing depression.
- The Department of Health (2001) reviewed studies of behavioural, cognitive, humanistic and psychotherapeutic treatments, finding CBT to be most effective, while Houghton *et al.* (2008) found that *behavioural activation therapy*, a behaviourist treatment, was effective, tolerable and incurred low drop-out rates, which suggests psychological treatments are appropriate.

Positive evaluation

✔ Patients could self-diagnose depression using internet-based self-assessments. Chao-Cheng et al. (2002) assessed the test-re-test reliability of such measures, finding a 75 per cent concordance rate, suggesting they are reliable.

✔ The most enduring biological theory of depression is that of the biochemical explanation, illustrating its appropriateness.

✔ CBT has few side effects and is regarded as the most effective psychological treatment for moderate and severe depressions. The idea of cognitive vulnerability upon which the treatment is based also has considerable research.

Psychological explanations include *behaviourist explanations*, perceiving depression as a learned response to environmental factors, with operant conditioning playing a key role. *Cognitive explanations* focus on maladaptive thought processes, where the world is perceived negatively, with such negative schemas causing a misperception of reality.

Biological therapies include *antidepressant drugs*, which stimulate monoamine neurotransmitters in the brain leading to physical arousal. Such drugs are effective, but incur serious side effects. *Electroconvulsive therapy* (ECT) involves a brief electric shock given to the brain to induce a seizure. Bilateral ECT is more effective than unilateral ECT, but incurs more side effects.

Psychological therapies include *cognitive behavioural therapy* (CBT), where irrational and maladaptive thoughts associated with an individual's depression are altered and *behavioural therapies*, which use operant conditioning and social learning techniques to elevate mood and encourage participation in positive behaviours. Both therapies have proved effective.

Negative evaluation

✘ Performing twin studies to evaluate the genetic explanation is affected by diagnostic unreliability, where if researchers know one twin is depressive it biases their assessment of whether the other twin is depressive.

✘ Side-effects of drug therapies include cerebral haemorrhage, toxic effects on the cardio-vascular system and violent behaviour. In addition, being lethal in overdose, they pose a risk of being used by suicidal depressives. Drugs also take time to act, making it difficult to get patients to continue taking them.

✘ Fluctuations in biochemistry may not be a cause, but an effect of depression.

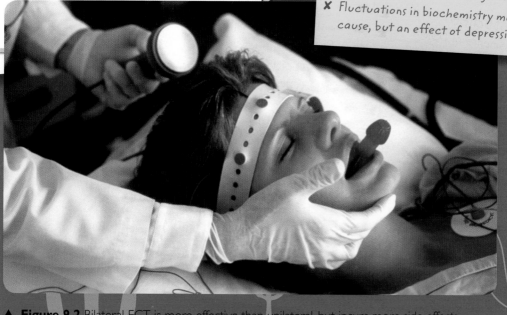

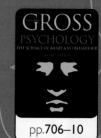

GROSS
PSYCHOLOGY
THE SCIENCE OF MIND AND BEHAVIOUR

pp.706–10

▲ **Figure 9.2** Bilateral ECT is more effective than unilateral, but incurs more side effects

PHOBIC DISORDERS

Focal study

Jones (1924) treated a two-year old boy called 'Little Peter', who exhibited, among other fears, a phobia of white fluffy animals and objects. Using rewards of food to develop a positive association, she put a rabbit in a wire cage in front of the boy while he ate his dinner. When Peter was at ease with that, the rabbit was presented at closer and closer distances each time his anxiety levels decreased sufficiently to permit movement to the next step. Eventually, after 40 SD sessions his conditioned fondness for the rabbit generalised onto similar animals and objects.

Description

Phobias involve extreme, irrational fear of specific objects or situations and are characterised by high levels of anxiety, fear of exposure to the phobic stimulus, recognition of exaggerated fear, avoidant/anxiety responses and disruption of functioning. Phobias divide into *simple phobias*, *social phobias* and *agoraphobia*, with simple phobias sub-dividing into *animal*, *injury*, *situational* and *natural environment* phobias.

Reliability of diagnosis through classification systems like DSM and ICD is high, though *validity* issues exist over sub-types being truly independent of each other.

With *biological explanations*, research involving twins, adoption and gene mapping studies suggest some *genetic* influence, while *evolutionary explanations* see phobias as having an adaptive value linked to survival.

With *psychological explanations*, research suggests a role for *behaviourism*, with phobias

Additional studies

- Original assessments of DSM measuring scales produced low levels of reliability for diagnosing phobias, while later assessments found higher levels of reliability. This suggests it was the revision of the scales that occurred during this time that led to greater reliability.
- Kendler *et al.* (1992) found a concordance rate of 24.4 per cent for social phobias in MZ twins, but only 15.3 per cent in DZ twins, suggesting a genetic component.
- Watson & Rayner (1920) demonstrated how a fear of white furry objects could be induced in 'Little Albert' by pairing the neutral stimulus of a white rat with the unconditioned stimulus of a loud noise, illustrating how phobias can develop via classical conditioning.
- Slaap *et al.* (1996) found that 72 per cent of social phobics had lower heart rate and blood pressure when treated with antidepressants, suggesting drug treatments are effective in treating phobias.
- Kvale *et al.* (2004) found that treating dental phobias with CBT resulted in 77 per cent of patients regularly visiting a dentist four years after treatment, emphasising the long-term effectiveness of the treatment.

Positive evaluation

✔ Biological and behaviourist explanations can be combined to explain how some individuals have greater genetic levels of vulnerability to developing phobias through environmental experiences.

✔ Cognitive explanations detail the thought processes underpinning phobias and thus are superior to behavioural experiences that concentrate only on visible behaviour.

✔ Modern day psychosurgery is less invasive and destructive, as it is targeted upon specific brain areas. This avoids large-scale brain tissue destruction, thus lowering the risks of irreversible side effects.

✔ As well as being proven an effective treatment, CBT produces few side effects and is long-term beneficial, as it can be utilised repeatedly to stop symptoms reappearing.

initiated through classical conditioning and then maintained via operant conditioning. *Cognitive explanations* see phobics as having an attentional bias whereby they over-focus on threatening stimuli and then maintain phobias by cognitively rehearsing fear reactions.

Biological therapies centre on anxiety reducing drugs, such as anxiolytics, beta blockers and anti-depressants, which are effective, but can incur side effects. *Psychosurgery* is occasionally used for phobias that are non-responsive to other treatments, but does not guarantee improvement and can incur serious side effects.

Psychological therapies focus on *behavioural treatments*, like systematic desensitisation (SD), based on classical conditioning, which uses a stage-by-stage approach to feared objects, where fear responses are replaced with feelings of calm. *Cognitive behavioural therapy* is the most common treatment and helps phobics to identify irrational, maladaptive thought processes underpinning phobias and replace them with rational, adaptive ones.

Negative evaluation

✗ Although family studies indicate a genetic component to phobias, related individuals may develop phobias due to similar environmental experiences, weakening support for the explanation.

✗ Some phobias are so unique and weird that it is difficult to see them as having an adaptive advantage and they are better explained as being learned through conditioned responses, lessening support for the evolutionary explanation.

✗ Not everyone experiencing traumatic events, like nearly drowning, goes on to develop phobias, refuting the behaviourist explanation.

▲ **Figure 9.3** Little Peter's fear of white fluffy animals was eradicated through systematic desensitisation

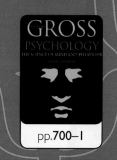

GROSS
PSYCHOLOGY
THE SCIENCE OF MIND AND BEHAVIOUR

pp.700–1

OBSESSIVE COMPULSIVE DISORDER (OCD)

Description

Obsessions involve forbidden or inappropriate ideas and visual images that create feelings of intense anxiety, while compulsions involve extreme, uncontrollable urges to repetitively perform behaviours. Suffers generally know their compulsions are inappropriate, but cannot consciously control them. Obsessions are characterised by thoughts that are *persistent and recurrent*, *irrelevant to real life*, *suppressed* and *recognised as self-generated*. Compulsions are characterised by being *repetitive* and *aimed at reducing distress*.

Classification systems, such as DSM and ICD, suggest that diagnosis is *reliable*, but may lack *validity* in not being a separate disorder and that diagnostic scales may need revising.

With *biological explanations*, research using twin and gene mapping studies suggests a genetic component, while *evolutionary explanations* perceive OCD as having an adaptive advantage linked to survival.

Additional studies

- Deacon & Abramovitz (2004) found that there were problems with the sub-scales of the Yale-Brown Obsessive-Compulsive Scale, the accepted diagnostic measure of OCD, in accurately measuring the components of the disorder, which suggests it lacks validity.

- Chepko-Sade et al. (1989) found that following within-group fighting, rhesus monkeys who carried out the most grooming of others were retained by the group, which suggests OCD has an adaptive advantage, supporting the evolutionary explanation.

- Meyer & Cheeser (1970) proposed that compulsions are responses learned via operant conditioning, which lower elevated anxiety levels incurred through obsessive behaviour, thus supporting a behaviourist explanation.

- Mallett et al. (2008) found that treatment of OCD by deep brain stimulation produced symptom reduction, demonstrating the treatment's effectiveness.

- Lindsay et al. (1997) found that ERP programmes produced noticeable improvements after three weeks of treatment, while anxiety management programmes did not, thus demonstrating the relative effectiveness of the treatment.

- Cordioli (2008) reviewed trials and meta-analyses of CBT to find that symptoms were reduced in 70 per cent of patients, providing support for the treatment.

Positive evaluation

✔ In assessing the reliability of diagnosis of anxiety disorders, the American Psychiatric Association (1987) reported the diagnostic reliability of OCD to be relatively high.

✔ Common behavioural components of OCD, such as hoarding and precision in behaviour, would have had an adaptive advantage in our evolutionary past and remain now due to genome lag.

✔ As CBT has proven an effective treatment of OCD by correcting cognitive bias and assisting sufferers in becoming less vigilant, it provides support for the cognitive explanation upon which OCD is based.

With *psychological explanations*, research suggests a role for behaviourism, with OCD initiated and maintained through operant conditioning. *Cognitive explanations* sees sufferers as possessing impaired, persistent thought processes, leading to self-blame and anxiety.

Biological therapies involve anxiety-reducing drugs, such as anxiolytics, antidepressants and beta-blockers, which are effective, but can incur side effects. *Psychosurgery* is occasionally used for OCD cases that are non-responsive to other treatments, but does not guarantee improvement and can incur serious side effects. Recently, deep-brain stimulation, which is less invasive and reversible, has been used.

Psychological therapies focus on behavioural treatments, like *exposure and response prevention* (ERP), where reinforcement of obsessive behaviour is prevented by denial of usual obsessive responses. *Cognitive behavioural therapy* (CBT) is targeted at altering obsessional cognitions by repeatedly re-experiencing obsessional thoughts to reduce anxiety levels.

▲ **Figure 9.4** OCD involves uncontrollable urges to perform repetitive actions

Negative evaluation

✘ Family studies indicate a genetic component to OCD, but do not reveal the mechanisms by which genetics would play a role, though gene mapping research may prove beneficial here.

✘ Research suggests that operant conditioning plays a role in the initiation and maintenance of OCD, but cannot explain a key feature, that of intrusive thoughts, weakening support for the behaviourist explanation.

✘ Once drug treatments cease, OCD symptoms can return, suggesting such treatments to be long-term ineffective.

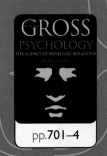

GROSS
PSYCHOLOGY
THE SCIENCE OF MIND AND BEHAVIOUR

pp.701–4

EXPLANATIONS OF SOCIAL INFLUENCES AND PRO- AND ANTI-SOCIAL BEHAVIOUR

Description

Media influences concern the effects of public forms of communication on pro- and anti-social behaviour. *Social learning theory* (SLT) sees learning via the media as occurring through indirect reinforcement, where observed behaviours seen to be rewarded, are imitated. In this manner the media teaches negative and positive consequences of aggression, but equally media depictions of pro-social actions have a similar impact on behaviour.

Cognitive priming occurs when individuals store anti-social and pro-social ideas or 'cues' in memory as 'scripts' for later behaviour, triggered by being in similar situations.

Desensitisation concerns the reduction or abolition of behavioural, emotional and cognitive responses to stimuli through repeated exposure to those stimuli. Therefore continual exposure to media violence lessens its impact as individuals become habituated to it. Similar over-exposure to pro-social media creates 'compassion fatigue', again lessening the impact of the message.

Additional studies

- Paik & Comstock (1994) found that if actors were seen to be reinforced for their behaviour then the imitative effects of TV violence on an audience were greater, illustrating how social learning through observation and imitation can lead to anti-social behaviour.
- Kestenbaum & Weinstein (1985) found that video games allow players to release stress and aggression in a non-destructive manner and lead to relaxation, demonstrating the positive effects of video game playing.
- Surrey (1982) found that computers give children access to state-of-the-art technology, which equips them with confidence and computer skills for adult life, again showing the positive aspects of computer usage.
- Drabman & Thomas (1974) found there was less emotional response and more tolerance of later aggression in children viewing violent films, which suggests a desensitisation effect.
- Pearce (2007) found that only 4 per cent of information presented via a computer screen was recalled, compared to 27 per cent presented via a film of printed paper and 85 per cent presented by printed paper. This implies that computers are a poor medium for learning.

Positive evaluation

✔ A common view is that media has more negative than positive effects, but anti-social acts are more obvious and easier to measure, while pro-social acts are subtler and difficult to assess, as they are based on value judgements. Therefore, the media may have more of an influence on pro-social behaviour than is first apparent.

✔ Research suggests that negative effects of video games are short lived, while positive effects have a greater, longer lasting impact, so that overall game playing can be regarded in a favourable light.

Video games exert an influence through repetitive learning experiences and by giving players active roles. They have negative qualities, like addiction tendencies, encouragement of and desensitisation to violence and retardation of development, but also include positive features, like their educational value, ability to raise self-esteem and stress-release qualities.

Computers are a continually growing source of media influence and have negative associations with dependency behaviours, deindividuation that leads to disinhibition, causing individuals to act in non-typical ways and their retardation of face-to-face social communication skills. However, on the positive side computers have great educational potential and allow social relationships in those lacking personal skills and confidence and those in remote communities.

Negative evaluation

✘ The correlation between amount of aggressive/pro-social TV watched and aggressive/pro-social behaviour may occur because aggressive/pro-social individuals choose to view more violent/helpful programmes.

✘ Griffiths (1997) argues that claims made for the positive attributes of video games and computers were subjectively made, having little, if any, research evidence to back them up.

✘ Prolonged use of computers can create disinhibition that makes users indifferent to the welfare of others, self-centred and lacking in real-life communication and social skills. This suggests that access to computer usage should have time limitations, especially for the young, who are still developing their communication and sociability skills.

▲ **Figure 10.1** Continual exposure to media violence lessens its impact

GROSS
PSYCHOLOGY
THE SCIENCE OF MIND AND BEHAVIOUR

pp.455–62; 478–9

HOVLAND-YALE AND THE ELABORATION LIKELIHOOD MODEL

Description

The *Hovland-Yale model* perceives attitude change as a response to communication through four factors:

1. *The communicator*, involving the person seeking to persuade.

2. *The message*, involving the content of the communication.

3. *The channel*, concerning how the message is conveyed.

4. *The audience*, concerning to whom the message is directed.

Overall, attitude change is perceived as a sequential series of stages involving *attention*, *comprehension*, *reactance* and *acceptance*.

The *Elaboration Likelihood model* focuses on cognitions rather than message content and details how persuasive messages are processed through *central routes* (CR) and *peripheral routes* (PR), with attitude change occurring via cognitive evaluation and persuasion dependent on the

Additional studies

- Hovland & Weiss (1951) investigating the Hovland-Yale model, found more attitude change was created in participants reading an article supposedly written by an expert, rather than a low-credibility source, suggesting that experts are more credible and persuasive than non-experts.

- Sinclair *et al.* (1991) investigating the Hovland-Yale model found a message given on a sunny day was more supported than that given on a cloudy day, regardless of the strength of the message, illustrating how the persuasiveness of messages are dependent on mood.

- Petty & Cacioppo (1986), investigating the Elaboration Likelihood model, found that as central processing involves more time and cognitive effort it creates longer-lasting attitude change than peripheral processing, demonstrating the CR to be a stronger form of persuasion.

- Belch (1982) found that attitudes and purchase intentions were unaffected by advertisement repetition and that cognitive responses grew negative as repetitions increased, which suggests advertisements are not persuasive and can create negativity towards products.

amount of elaboration of messages. The CR is utilised when receivers have both the motivation and ability to think about messages and is characterised by *persuasive communication*, *motivation to process*, *ability to process* and the *nature of argument*. The PR is used when messages do not impact through the CR, as the audience cannot engage due to simultaneous conflicting demands and is characterised by *consistency, likeability, expertise and authority* and *scarcity*.

The *hypodermic effect* perceives television advertising as injecting its message into a targeted audience, who are passive recipients and easily persuaded, while the *two-step flow theory* perceives the messages within television advertisements as being filtered through influential opinion leaders who pass the information onto others. The *uses and gratification theory* sees people as active processors using television advertisements to fulfil their needs, with advertisements interacting with their audience to produce an effect.

Positive evaluation

✔ Research upon the Hovland-Yale model revealed factors important in persuasion and attitude change, which have been effectively incorporated into advertisements, speech-writing and so forth.

✔ The Elaboration Likelihood model is the most influential explanation of persuasion, as it acknowledges that similar messages can be processed via different cognitive routes, reliant upon whether individuals have the motivation and ability to use active or passive processing methods.

✔ Television advertising in the form of public safety campaigns have proven to be most effective when they are targeted at specific audiences, especially the 2–3 per cent of people perceived as opinion makers and agents of social change, because they then have a knock-on effect on others, which supports the two-step flow theory.

▲ **Figure 10.2** Messages from experts are more persuasive than those from non-experts

Negative evaluation

✗ The Hovland-Yale model does not identify how persuasion occurs and has an assumption that attitude change comes from message comprehension, which research suggests is not always so.

✗ Research into the Elaboration Likelihood model tends to measure attitude change rather than attitude formation, as most research involved unfamiliar topics where no pre-existing attitudes exist.

✗ It is difficult to assess if TV advertising is effective, as most research is conducted by advertising agencies who keep their findings private.

SOCIAL, PSYCHOLOGICAL AND EVOLUTIONARY EXPLANATIONS OF THE ATTRACTIVENESS OF CELEBRITY

Focal study

De Backer (2007) investigated two compatible hypotheses:

- The *learning hypothesis*, which perceives interest in celebrity gossip as a by-product of an evolved mechanism for accumulating survival-increasing information.

- The *parasocial hypothesis*, which views celebrity gossip as a misperception of celebrities being part of one's social network. A survey of 838 participants and 103 in-depth interviews revealed that the younger a participant was, the more they thought they learned from celebrities, while as participants aged, the more they saw celebrities as friends, supporting both hypotheses and giving support to social psychological and evolutionary explanations.

Description

Social psychological explanations of the attractiveness of celebrity include *social learning theory* (SLT), which perceives celebrities as acting as role models to observe and imitate due to the belief that doing so will incur similar popularity and success. The relationships that people have with celebrities are *parasocial relationships* – one-sided relationships that occur outside of a person's actual social network – though they may be misperceived as real. Zajonc's (1968) *mere exposure effect* theorises that repeated exposure to celebrities leads to people finding them attractive, comforting and trustworthy.

Personality factors may be involved too, with certain personality types having a greater need for fame and thus an association with the famous. Research also suggests that people from impoverished backgrounds are attracted to celebrity, as they associate fame with being wanted and accepted.

Additional studies

- Freeman et al. (1978) found that repeated exposure to celebrities who had personalities, interests and opinions different to that of participants made those participants dislike them even more. This implies Zajonc's mere exposure effect only works with 'agreeable' celebrities by confirming the attraction to them.

- Giles (2000) reported that there was an abnormally high number of Jewish Nobel prize winners and black sports people and pop musicians. As such people come from disadvantaged cultural backgrounds it suggests they are attracted to becoming celebrities as a means of escaping their impoverished origins and gaining self-esteem and respect.

- Fieldman (2008) found that male celebrities are attractive to females, as they exhibit toughness, stamina and high levels of testosterone: all qualities indicative of good genes and resource richness, thus supporting the evolutionary explanation.

- Reynolds (2009) argued that celebrities are regarded as universally popular, because evolution programmes people to find qualities that advertise good genetic fitness as attractive and it is these qualities that celebrities display, again supporting the evolutionary explanation.

Evolutionary explanations see the attractiveness of celebrity as serving an adaptive function linked to survival, with people becoming celebrities to get better access to resources. Interest in celebrity journalism allows people to keep up to date with news of alpha males and females who possess qualities important to survival and reproduction. Individuals benefit from possession of such information, as it helps strengthen relationships and elevates status. Celebrity females are often physically attractive and youthful, while male celebrities are resource-rich, qualities associated with increased reproduction opportunities. Celebrity interest also allows people to compare themselves in levels of attractiveness and learn attractiveness skills. There is also a benefit in imitating celebrities, as it may incur more resources and increased reproduction opportunities.

▲ **Figure 10.3** Celebrity through sport is a means of escaping a disadvantaged background for black people

Negative evaluation

✘ The obsession with celebrity, constantly fuelled by the media, has negative implications, as people may come to believe that only by achieving similar fame and fortune can happiness and life satisfaction be reached. In addition, celebrity photographs, especially those of females, are often doctored and thus present unattainable standards of beauty that may be contributing to escalating levels of anorexia nervosa.

✘ Evolutionary explanations see celebrity as something that those attaining it have aspired to. However, many celebrities attain fame reluctantly, with no conscious desire or effort to do so, which goes against evolutionary theory.

RESEARCH INTO INTENSE FANDOM

Description

Celebrity worship is characterised by several factors. It occurs at all ages, but peaks between 11–17 years of age and then declines slowly thereafter. There is a gender difference, in that females are more focused on the entertainment world, while males concentrate more on sports stars. Level of education is another factor, with a negative correlation evident of the less education one receives, the more interest in celebrity. This may occur because highly educated individuals perceive most celebrities as less educated and therefore not worthy of hero worship. The Celebrity Attitude Scale (CAS) was developed to provide reliable measures of celebrity interest and revealed that most people's interest in celebrities is based on their entertainment value. However, some people develop *celebrity worship syndrome*,

Additional studies

- Maltby et al. (2003) found three dimensions of fandom: entertainment social, where people are attracted to celebrities for entertainment value, intense-personal, where people develop obsessive tendencies towards celebrities and borderline pathological, where people develop uncontrollable fantasies and behaviour patterns. This suggests fandom differs in its intensity.

- McCutcheon et al. (2002) found a negative correlation between the level of education achieved by participants and the degree to which they idolised celebrities. This suggests that interest in celebrity is linked to the amount of education received.

- McCutcheon et al. (2006) found that participants with insecure attachment types had positive attitudes concerning obsessive tendencies towards celebrities and the stalking of them. An association between pathological attachment types and stalking was also found, suggesting a link between the behaviour and childhood attachment patterns.

- Mullen (2008) found of 20,000 incidents of stalking members of the Royal family, 80 per cent were by individuals with psychotic disorders. This is very different to the stalking of non-celebrities and suggests celebrity stalking is a separate phenomena.

Positive evaluation

✓ Larsen (1995) argued that mild forms of celebrity worship are actually beneficial, as intense attachments to celebrities give young people positive attitudinal and behavioural models to emulate.

✓ Research into celebrity stalking is essential in order to understand the phenomena, so that effective therapies and strategies can be developed. Currently psychotherapy is used to attend to underlying causes, while drug treatments are also used against the obsessive tendencies of stalkers.

✓ Using relationship counselling to help achieve satisfactory relationship terminations can help to stop resentments forming that develop into stalking behaviour.

a condition characterised by obsessive interest in celebrities that is parasocial, where individuals perceive themselves as truly having a relationship with celebrities.

Such intense fandom can be fairly harmless, but for some it becomes delusional and pathological and spills over into celebrity stalking, defined as '*the wilful, malicious and repeated following or harassing of another person that threatens his or her safety*'. Most stalkers are male, with high levels of criminality, drug use and mental illness, and most victims female, but there is no overall single type. The development of valid measuring scales like the Obsessive Relational Intrusion and Celebrity Stalking Scale has aided research and recently a link has been identified between stalking and insecure attachment types, as well as personal loss preceding stalking behaviour.

Negative evaluation

✗ Much research in this area relies on questionnaires, which are prone to idealised and socially desirable answers. Findings also tend to be in the form of correlations, which do not show cause and effect relationships.

✗ Trespassing orders and similar legal interventions tend currently to be used against celebrity stalkers, but these can backfire by making perpetrators become even more malicious, obsessive and persecutory in their behaviour.

✗ Psychotherapy is quite effective when used with non-celebrity stalkers, but much less so with celebrity stalkers, which again suggests celebrity stalking is a separate condition.

▲ **Figure 10.4** Celebrity worship syndrome is characterised by obsessive interest in celebrities

MODELS OF ADDICTIVE BEHAVIOUR

Description

The *biological model* of addiction sees dependency as physiologically controlled, initiation of addiction being determined by genetic vulnerability triggered by environmental stressors, with maintenance of addiction regulated through activation of dopamine. Relapse occurs through physiological cravings, with research indicating that brain circuitry regulating survival behaviours is activated by such cravings. Addicts are perceived as having an impaired *pre-frontal cortex* that does not stop them pursuing damaging reinforcements. Increased dopamine production also results in *desensitisation*, where higher doses are required to achieve satisfaction.

The *cognitive model* perceives dependency as due to distorted thinking, like believing happiness only occurs through addictive

Additional studies

- Leshner & Koob (1999) reported that the nucleus accumbus brain area is the 'universal addiction site', as most, if not all, drugs and dependency behaviours stimulate extracellular dopamine in this area, which supports the biological model of addiction.

- Koski-Jannes (1992) found that addictions originate from ways of dealing with stressors that give short-term positive results, but incur long-term negative consequences. This creates a self-generated, repeating cycle of dependency behaviour regulated via self-serving thinking. This supports a cognitive explanation of addiction initiation.

- Meyer et al. (1995) found positive sensations occurred in addicts at the sight of a syringe, illustrating how classical conditioning contributes to dependency. The learning model was further supported by White & Hiroi (1993) finding rats preferred locations where they previously received amphetamines, demonstrating the role of operant conditioning. Bahr et al. (2005) reported that drug taking by peers influenced dependency behaviour in adolescents, showing how SLT also plays a part.

- Grant et al. (1996) found that during periods of cravings there was increased activity in the prefrontal cortex, a brain area associated with decision making, which implies the cognitive and biological models can be combined to explain dependency behaviours.

behaviours. Such beliefs lead to a mind set of personal incapability to control dependency behaviours and an inability to direct attention away from them. Positive features of dependency behaviours are focused on, while negative ones are ignored, strengthening dependency. Relapse occurs if addicts perceive themselves as lacking the motivation to quit and disbelieving in coping strategies and their personal capacity to resist.

Learning models perceive various behavioural processes as linked to dependency behaviours. *Classical conditioning* sees addictions occurring through an unconditioned stimulus that produces a natural response of pleasure becoming associated with a conditioned stimulus that does not, to produce the same response. *Operant conditioning* sees dependency behaviours as positively reinforcing through the pleasure they create and negatively reinforcing through the cravings they reduce. *Social learning theory* (SLT) perceives dependencies as emanating from vicarious learning where addictive behaviours are observed and imitated if a model is seen to be reinforced for such behaviours.

Positive evaluation

✔ The success of cognitive behavioural therapy suggests that dependency behaviours are best explained by the cognitive model.

✔ A wealth of evidence based on twin, family and gene mapping studies suggests that there is a biological predisposition to addiction.

✔ Classical conditioning is able to explain how stimuli associated with dependencies, like drugs paraphernalia, produce similar pleasurable responses to dependency behaviours themselves.

Negative evaluation

✘ The biological model relies upon research produced from animal experimentation, which produces problems of generalisation to humans where dependency behaviours may have more of a cognitive component to them.

✘ Cognitive explanations of dependency are incomplete, being based on expectations and beliefs and thus neglecting the important role of biological factors. For instance, although the cognitive model is well able to explain maintenance of dependency and relapses, the biological model is better able to explain initiation of addiction.

✘ Treatments based on behaviourism do not provide long-term cures, which suggests underlying causes are not addressed.

Nucleus accumbens

▲ **Figure 11.1** The nucleus accumbuns brain area is regarded as the universal addiction site

GROSS
PSYCHOLOGY

pp.113–14;
124–5; 116–17

THE APPLICATION OF MODELS OF ADDICTION TO SMOKING AND GAMBLING

Focal study

deCODE genetics (2008) assessed the association between specific gene variants and smoking behaviour. A survey of 50,000 Icelanders who completed a smoking history questionnaire asked if participants had ever smoked, were still smoking and, if so, how many cigarettes a day were smoked. Over 300,000 single-letter variants of the human genome were analysed in a sub-set of over 10,000 smokers. A common variant in the nicotinic acetylcholine receptor gene cluster on chromosome 15q24 was found that was related to the number of cigarettes smoked daily and with nicotine dependency. It was concluded that there is a genetic link to smoking addiction.

Description

Biological explanations see smoking as affecting production of the neurotransmitters *dopamine* and *acetylcholine* through stimulation of nicotine receptors in the brain, producing a pleasurable effect in the brain reward system. Neurochemical changes cause desensitisation, leading to increased tolerance and maintenance of smoking. Abstinence creates physiological cravings due to non-stimulation of dopamine receptors, leading to relapses.

Cognitive explanations see smokers possessing irrational thoughts, like believing smoking improves concentration. Such dysfunctional ideas become self-fulfilling, creating a repeating cycle of giving in to cravings.

Learning explanations see initiation of smoking as best explained through social learning theory (SLT) by the observation and imitation of models through vicarious reinforcement, while operant

Additional studies

- NIDA (2005) reported that 90 per cent of American smokers started in adolescence, mainly due to observing and imitating peers, suggesting that SLT was responsible for initiation.
- Goldberg et al. (1981) found that smoking was maintained in monkeys through its reinforcing effect, as monkeys pressed a lever to receive nicotine at a similar rate as for cocaine, which implies operant conditioning was responsible.
- Anholt et al. (2003) found evidence of obsessive-compulsive thinking in dependent gamblers, supporting a cognitive explanation.
- Roy et al. (2004) found higher dopamine levels in chronic casino gamblers and higher noradrenaline levels in chronic blackjack players that suggests a biological explanation for addiction.
- Clark et al. (2009) found that gambling near-misses were seen as 'special events', with heightened brain activity occurring in the striatum and insula cortex – areas receiving dopamine input – which are associated with other types of dependency. This suggests that cognitive, learning and biological explanations can be combined to explain gambling dependency.

conditioning explains maintenance of smoking behaviour through constant reinforcements.

Biological explanations perceive gambling as increasing dopamine and other neurotransmitter production, creating pleasurable sensations in the brain reward system, while cortisol levels are also increased. Genes appear to determine genetic vulnerability to gambling dependency, as well as exerting influence over personality factors linked to gambling addiction, such as impulsivity, high sensation-seeking and susceptibility to boredom.

Cognitive explanations perceive dependent gamblers as possessing irrational thoughts and distorted views concerning luck and skill and the development of superstitious beliefs to account for winning and losing that lead to increased risk taking and persistence.

Learning explanations sees SLT accounting for initiation of gambling dependency by observation and imitation of role models through vicarious reinforcement, while operant conditioning explains maintenance of gambling dependency through a variable-ratio schedule of unpredictable reinforcing wins.

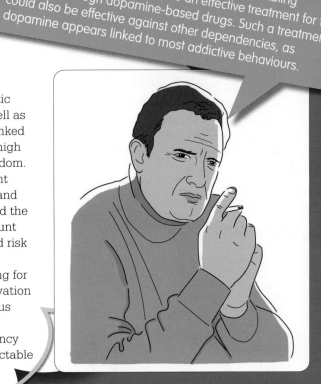

▲ **Figure 11.2** Cognitive explanations see smokers as possessing irrational thoughts such as 'concentration is not possible without smoking'

Focal study

Block (2008) investigated the risks of internet addiction disorder (IAD). Using data provided by the South Korean government it was found that IAD is one of the most serious public health issues; 210,000 children aged 6–19 are afflicted to the extent they require treatment (2.1 per cent of that age group). Of those requiring treatment, 80 per cent need psychotropic medicines and 24 per cent need hospitalisation. Since the average South Korean high school student spends 23 hours a week on computer games, which has a serious affect on work output, it is believed another 1.2 million are at risk of addiction and require counselling. The findings show the severity and increasing nature of IAD.

Description

Individuals have different levels of vulnerability to addiction, with both biological and environmental factors contributing to vulnerability levels.

Personality is one such factor, with neurotic and psychopathic personality types especially at risk, though research does not support the existence of an addictive personality.

Peers affect vulnerability, especially during adolescence, through normative social influence. This is where individuals conform to dependency behaviours to be accepted and through operant conditioning, where dependency behaviours are reinforced by the group.

Age also affects vulnerability, with early onset of dependency behaviours linked to reduced likelihood of abstaining and increased likelihood of developing other addictions. There is increased vulnerability too during old age, possibly due to increased stressors and lifestyle changes.

Additional studies

- Chein et al. (1964) found that adolescent ghetto addicts had a negative outlook on life, characterised by low self-esteem, learned incompetence, passivity and dependent relationships, which suggests personality factors increase vulnerability to addiction.

- Sussman & Ames (2001) found that peer group use of drugs was a good predictor of drug use in adolescents, illustrating how peers affect vulnerability to dependency through social learning theory via observation and imitation.

- Griffiths (1997) reported that more people from lower class than middle and upper class backgrounds participated in national lotteries around the world. Since people from the lower classes watch more television it suggests that media influences, in the form of television marketing of such lotteries, has a marked impact on gambling behaviour.

- Gunsekera et al. (2005) reported that drug-taking in movies was characterised in a positive way and that little reference to negative consequences was made, which supports the idea that the media promotes dependency behaviours and misrepresents their dangers.

Positive evaluation

✔ As recovered addicts often develop dependencies on non-harmful and beneficial behaviours, like religion and fitness regimes, it supports the notion that personality is linked to vulnerability to addiction.

✔ Public health initiatives that seek to address dependency behaviours are more effective if they are specifically targeted at specific age groups, such as the young and the elderly, as they are particularly vulnerable to developing addictions.

✔ The media can also exert positive influences concerning addiction, such as using positive role models who abstain from dependency behaviours, as well by educational means through truly representing the dangers of indulging in such behaviours.

Stress is positively correlated with vulnerability to dependency and the stress produced by attempting to maintain abstinence can lead to relapse.

The *media* communicates information about addictive behaviours through public formats, affecting individual's perceptions and behaviour towards dependency. The media is also accused of presenting role models who promote positive images of addictive behaviours, which can exert a harmful effect through observation and imitation of such models. In addition, the media is accused of misrepresenting the risks of addiction through indulging in dependency behaviours, which influences individuals to participate in such behaviours, as they underestimate the chances of addiction. There is also the growing phenomenon of psychological dependency to media itself, through the expanding provision of ever more forms of social media, such as television, mobile phones and social networking sites.

Negative evaluation

✘ Evidence linking stress to vulnerability to dependency is correlational and does not show causality. It may be that increased stress is an effect of being addicted, rather than a cause of dependency.

✘ Social media addiction is an increasing problem in the workplace. Farber (2007) reported that many employees display a persistent need to access social media sites, demonstrating how addiction to media has negative effects.

✘ If addicts are demonised in the media, it negatively affects their chances of receiving the social support necessary to assist them quitting.

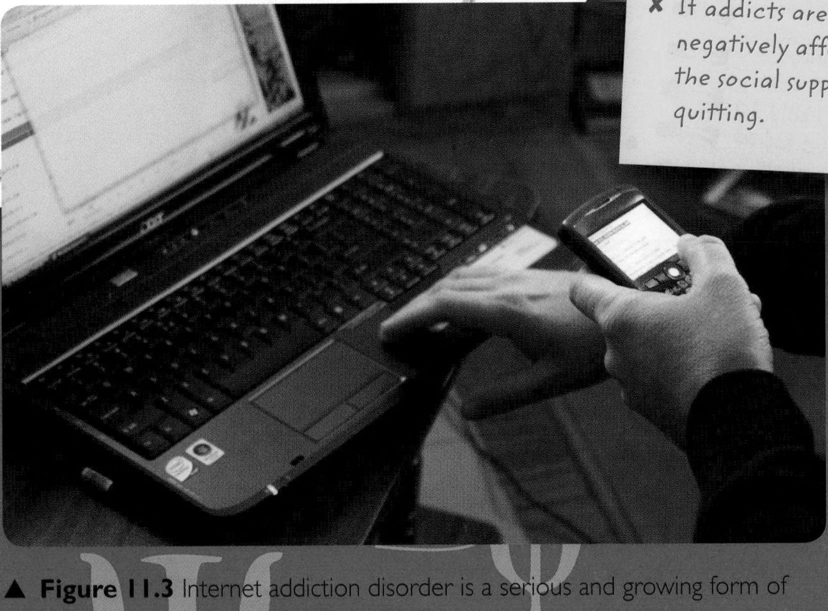

▲ **Figure 11.3** Internet addiction disorder is a serious and growing form of addiction

THEORY OF PLANNED BEHAVIOUR AND TYPES OF INTERVENTION AND THEIR EFFECTIVENESS

Description

The theory of planned behaviour (TPB) is an extension of the theory of reasoned action, which sees attempts to abstain from dependency behaviours as due to factors supporting decision making, rather than predisposing factors. However, TPB has an added component where addicts need confidence in their abilities and available resources to quit. TPB has three components:

1. *Behavioural beliefs*, involving the subjective probability that behaviour will produce abstention.

2. *Normative beliefs*, involving the degree of perceived social pressure to quit.

3. *Control beliefs*, involving individual beliefs about the ability to abstain.

TPB assesses an individual's motives for continuing dependency and their resolve to abstain. The higher their level of perceived behavioural control, the more likely they will quit.

Additional studies

- Penny (1996) found participants less likely to believe they will quit smoking and therefore less likely to try, the more times they have failed to quit previously. This illustrates the importance of past behaviour in determining perceived behavioural control, as predicted by TPB.

- Walsh & White (2007) measured TPB constructs of attitude, subjective norms and perceived behavioural control in students demonstrating high mobile phone use, finding that predictions of intentions and behaviour based on the model matched actual mobile phone use.

- Moore et al. (2009) found that nicotine replacement therapies were successful in attaining sustained abstinence from smoking in those who could not immediately abstain, demonstrating the effectiveness of biological interventions.

- Meyer & Chesser (1970) found that with aversion therapy 50 per cent of alcoholics abstained for at least a year and that the treatment was more successful than no treatment, giving support to interventions based on classical conditioning.

- Petry et al. (2000) found that CM was more successful in addressing alcoholism than intensive outpatient treatment, with only 26 per cent of CM patients relapsing compared to 61 per cent of the controls. This again gives support to the learning model, this time through operant conditioning.

With *types of intervention*, the main *biological treatment* is drug therapy, which assists with cravings and withdrawal symptoms and is more effective when combined with cognitive behavioural therapy.

Psychological interventions include those based on the *learning model*, like *aversion therapy* based on *classical conditioning* and *contingency management* (CM) based on operant conditioning.

Cognitive interventions focus on identification and elimination of false beliefs so that willpower is increased to give greater control over dependencies.

Public health interventions promote change in whole groups and work best when targeted at vulnerable groups. Techniques include *social inoculation*, providing counterarguments and supportive self-statements to resist temptation, *fear arousal*, strengthening the persuasiveness of arguments against dependencies and *targeting risk groups*, aimed at identifying and focusing on the vulnerable. Public health interventions occur through *medical advice*, *the workplace*, *community-based programmes* and *government interventions* (such as the smoking ban).

Positive evaluation

✔ TPB considers the important factors of irrationality, in the form of evaluation, and focuses on social and environmental factors through normative beliefs. The component of perceived behavioural control also allows for consideration of past behaviour.

✔ Cognitive behavioural therapy is relatively brief and long lasting, cheap enough to suit the financial capabilities of most health authorities. It can be tailored to individual needs and can even be effective with severely addicted persons.

✔ Public health interventions work best when based on models of behaviour change, like TPB.

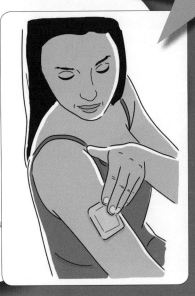

▲ **Figure 11.4** The success of nicotine replacement therapies suggests a biological explanation to smoking addiction

Negative evaluation

✘ TPB neglects the factor of anticipated regret, the strength of emotional disappointment if abstention is not realised, demonstrating the model's deficiencies in predicting actual behaviour.

✘ Drugs used against addiction incur side effects, for example, Varenicline, which is used against smoking dependency, can result in depression and suicide.

✘ A problem with therapies based on operant conditioning is getting addicts to use the techniques without clinical supervision.

✘ Identifying at-risk groups to be targeted by public health interventions can be expensive, thus reducing the cost-effectiveness of such intervention.

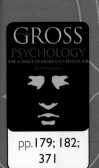

GROSS
PSYCHOLOGY
THE SCIENCE OF MIND AND BEHAVIOUR
SIXTH EDITION

pp. 179; 182; 371

Focal study

Honorton & Ferrari (1989) investigated the possible existence of ESP. A meta-analysis was performed of 309 ganzfeld studies, conducted by 62 separate researchers, over 52 years, involving 2 million trials from 50,000 participants. Each study was scored for the quality of its controls. A statistically significant effect was found, with studies involving participants demonstrating prior ability producing bigger effects and those testing individuals rather than groups. It was concluded that ESP abilities do exist and were tested for under conditions of scientific rigour, but that moderating effects may have occurred in some studies, like providing feedback after each trial.

Description

Pseudoscience refers to alleged sciences and scientific practices of no scientific basis. Many sceptics see anomalistic psychology – the study of extraordinary phenomena – as being pseudoscientific, misleading the public into believing false claims, like the existence of ghosts. Parapsychology is the scientific study of paranormal phenomena and has evolved from Victorian spiritualism to a discipline characterised by strict scientific rigour and objectivity. However, sceptics perceive paranormal phenomena as scientifically impossible and reject the legitimacy of parapsychology. Many see this rejection of psychic phenomena as scientifically inappropriate and believe that the possibility of evidence for their existence must not be rejected. Some parapsychologists argue that the case for paranormal phenomena is already proven.

Additional studies

- Honorton & Bem (1994) found that autoganzfeld studies, conducted under strict controls without human intervention to prevent accidental information transference, replicated the significant findings of earlier studies, suggesting that ESP is an actuality.

- Milton & Wiseman (1999) found no significant effect from a meta-analysis of 30 ganzfeld studies. However, Palmer (2001) criticised them for using non-standard methods and repeated the meta-analysis with the standard procedure to find a significant result, thus illustrating the problem in getting sceptics and believers to agree on findings.

- Nelson & Radin (1989) found, from a meta-analysis of 832 PK experiments, a significant effect. This was supported by Jahn et al. (2005), who conducted over 1,000 experiments involving millions of trials to again find a significant effect, which suggests that under certain conditions PK effects are real.

- Hansel (1989) reported that when strict criteria for PK studies were applied, like the use of randomised targets and independent recorders, no study produced a significant effect. This implies that flawed methodology is responsible for apparent PK effects.

Positive evaluation

✔ It is important to have a clear demarcation between science and pseudoscience, as the wrongful acceptance of pseudoscientific claims could lead to inefficient and dangerous practical applications.

✔ The development of the ganzfeld technique and the even stricter autoganzfeld technique has benefited Psychology as a whole by providing rigorously controlled, unbiased research methodologies that can be used across many psychological fields.

✔ Rao & Palmer (1987) argue that the use of PK studies conducted under conditions of strict, randomised, machine-generated, non-human influenced control, provide conclusive evidence for the existence of the phenomenon.

Honorton (1974) developed the ganzfeld technique to assess extra-sensory perception (ESP) where a receiver, under conditions of sensory deprivation, attempts to telepathically receive one of four images 'communicated' by a sender. Significant results were claimed, but sceptics found procedural flaws that led to tighter controls. Significant results were again claimed by believers of ESP, but sceptics generally fail to replicate such findings.

Psychokinesis (PK) is the process of moving and/or affecting objects mentally with no physical contact. Macro-PK involves large effects, like spoon-bending, while micro-PK involves small effects, like influencing dice throws. Bio-PK involves influencing living systems. Like with ESP, PK research involves strict controls involving an automated protocol with random targets determined by machines and results recorded without human intervention to make bias and fraud an impossibility. Significant results are claimed, which sceptics continue to oppose.

Negative evaluation

✘ Pseudoscience obstructs proper science by promoting desirable ideas to a gullible public that fulfil powerful emotional needs neglected by mainstream sciences, like being able to communicate with departed loved ones.

✘ Although sceptics agree that ganzfeld experiments do not involve fraud, there is still the possibility of researcher bias influencing results, as findings tend to match researchers' beliefs.

✘ Parapsychologists believe that mainstream Psychology is biased against them, as the standard of proof required for parapsychological studies to be considered valid is higher than for other psychological areas.

▲ **Figure 12.1** Macro-psychokinesis involves large-effects, like spoon-bending

COINCIDENCE AND PROBABILITY JUDGEMENTS

Focal study

Wiseman et al. (1995) assessed the reliability of eyewitness testimony to phenomena witnessed at séances. Twenty-five participants completed a questionnaire measuring whether they believed paranormal events occur during séances. Participants attended three séances where a slate, a bell, a book and a table covered in luminous paint remain stationary, while participants try to mentally move a luminous ball suspended above the table. Of the participants, 27 per cent recalled at least one stationary object moving in the first two séances, 46 per cent of believers and 24 per cent of sceptics recalled the ball moving, while 40 per cent of believers and 14 per cent of sceptics recalled at least one other item moving. Twenty per cent of believers and 0 per cent of the sceptics thought they had witnessed real paranormal events. It was concluded that eyewitness testimony in séances is unreliable and more unreliable in believers than sceptics.

Description

A *coincidence* occurs through a cognitive bias of perceiving unrelated accidental events as causal, with the perception of coincidence leading to superstitions and fatalism, where events are seen as predestined and uncontrollable. Coincidences also arise because of short-cuts in information processing in an attempt to simplify understanding.

Probability judgements concern how people misjudge the probability of unrelated events being connected, seeing instead such events as being affected by paranormal influence, like believing that dreams come true. There are several cognitive factors involved in people's misperceptions of probability judgements that explain why coincidences are misperceived as paranormal forces:

● *Intuitive thinking styles*, concerning individuals who lack reasoning and critical evaluation of events, such that they believe

Additional studies

● Falk (1982) found that when weird coincidences happen, individuals tend to overemphasise such events as meaningful and ignore other non-confirmatory examples, demonstrating a bias in cognitive processing.

● Zsune & Jones (1989) calculated that the apparently significant event of thinking about a person five minutes before learning of their death would actually occur in America 3,000 times a year, illustrating how seemingly paranormal events can be explained logically.

● Esgate & Groome (2001) found that the number of people required for there to be a 1 in 2 chance of two people sharing a birthday was underestimated, demonstrating how people miscalculate the probability of events occurring.

● Genovese (2005) found that beliefs in the paranormal correlated with cognitive errors and intuitive thinking styles, suggesting cognitive factors affect paranormal beliefs.

● Blackmore & Troscianko (1985) found that believers in the paranormal were poorer at generating random numbers, which implies that believers are affected by cognitive illusions that lessen ability to assess the probability of events.

Positive evaluation

✔ The misperception of unrelated events being meaningful may occur because the calculation of whether events are coincidental or not is reliant upon accurate and full memory. As memory is reconstructive and prone to recall errors, wishful thinking and suggestion, accurate memory may not consistently occur, leading to the misperception of coincidental events.

✔ There may be an adaptive advantage explicable by evolutionary means in having a cognitive system that detects patterns and meaning in unrelated events. Such a system could function as a biological device that attempts to make sense of the world, making it more predictable and thus safer.

thoughts can influence events and that biological processes have intentions and goals, like believing willpower can cure ill health.

- *Cognitive illusions*, concerning a perceptual style where chance and probability are misperceived so that unseen psychic forces are seen at work. Such individuals have a poor understanding of randomness, reading significance into random patterns.

- *Illusion of control*, where believers in the paranormal perceive random processes as under personal control.

- *Confirmatory bias*, where evidence refuting the paranormal is ignored, while confirmatory evidence is overemphasised.

- *Cold reading*, where vague, general statements are seen as accurately describing a particular individual, such as the reading of horoscopes.

$$7\,{}^{9}2\,{}^{3}2\,{}^{6}4$$

▲ **Figure 12.2** Believers in the paranormal are poorer at generating random numbers

Negative evaluation

✘ Research does not indicate whether the cognitive factors identified as being involved in paranormal beliefs, such as illusion of control and confirmatory bias, are innate or learned, which suggests full comprehension of the topic has not been realised.

✘ Studies into the assessment of probability estimation produce conflicting results, with some showing that sceptics are better at making such estimates than believers, while other studies indicate no such difference. This suggests that either the area is not fully understood or that methodological flaws have occurred.

PERSONALITY FACTORS AND EXPLANATIONS FOR SUPERSTITION AND MAGICAL THINKING

Description

Superstitions are irrational beliefs that objects, actions or circumstances not logically related to a course of events influence outcomes. Superstitions are associated with magical thinking and ritual behaviours, which if adhered to are seen as guaranteeing desired results. They self-deceive individuals into believing that they have control over events and may involve personality factors, as they are most apparent in those with a high need for certainty. Superstitions are also explicable by operant conditioning and can be socio-cultural constructions passed on from one generation to another.

Magical thinking involves believing the mind to have a direct influence on events through channelled energy forces that serve to represent culturally specific and culturally universal

Additional studies

- Fluke et al. (2010) found three reasons for believing in superstitions: to gain control over uncertainty, to decrease helplessness and that a belief in superstitions is easier to rely on than coping strategies. This suggests superstitions have several functions.
- Skinner found that pigeons associated specific body movements with reinforcements of food, demonstrating how superstitions can be learned via operant conditioning.
- Irwin (1994) found a stronger belief in magical thinking, witchcraft, superstition and precognition in those who had an alcoholic parent in childhood, which suggests that such beliefs serve a coping function.
- Wiseman & Watt (2004) found that neuroticism was positively correlated with a belief in the paranormal, which implies that personality is linked to anomalous experience.
- Haraldsson & Houtkooper (1992) found a negative correlation between defensiveness and ESP ability, which suggests that defensive individuals feel threatened by ESP and thus block it out. This was supported by Watt & Morris (1995) who assessed defensiveness through people's reactions to weak sensory stimuli, to find defensive participants had lower defensiveness scores.

symbolism. Magical thinking therefore exists as a shared belief system, uniting people within cultural groupings. It involves *the law of similarity*, where events resembling each other are perceived as connected in a causal way that defies scientific investigation, and *the law of contagion*, which sees things that have been in contact with each other, as retaining their connections when separated.

Personality factors have been investigated to assess their role in anomalous experience, with *neuroticism* perceived as associated with beliefs in the paranormal, possibly because, as with superstitions and magical thinking, they decrease anxiety. *Defensiveness*, where there is cognitive resistance to perceiving situations and information as threatening, is also linked to anomalous experience, while *extroversion* has been specifically linked to the possession of ESP abilities.

▲ **Figure 12.3** Magical thinking is evident in the belief that red pills incur cardio-vascular effects through their colour association with blood

Negative evaluation

✘ Superstitions, through their ritualised nature, have an obsessive element that can contribute to the development of obsessive compulsive disorder, which is classified as a serious mental disorder that negatively affects the quality of sufferers' lives.

✘ It is easy to misperceive the relationship between personality factors and anomalous experience, as different personality factors are associated with different aspects of the paranormal. For example, neuroticism is linked with paranormal beliefs, while extroversion is specifically linked with ESP.

✘ Magical thinking can incur negative effects by people refusing effective medicines in favour of those based on magical thinking.

EXPLANATIONS AND RESEARCH CONCERNING PSYCHIC HEALING, OBES AND NDES AND PSYCHIC MEDIUMSHIP

Focal study

Benson et al. (2006) assessed whether prayer influences health. Patients receiving a coronary heart by-pass were randomly assigned to three groups, with 604 receiving prayers (having been told they may or may not receive prayers), 597 not receiving prayers (having been told they may or may not receive prayers) and 601 receiving prayers after being told they would. In groups uncertain about receiving prayers, complications occurred in 52 per cent who did receive prayers compared to 51 per cent of those who did not. Of those certain of receiving prayers, 59 per cent developed complications compared to 52 per cent of those uncertain of receiving prayers. It was concluded that praying had no effect on recovery.

Description

Psychic healing involves restoration of health through spiritual practices, often by physical contact (known as therapeutic touch), though psychic healing also occurs without physical contact and over large distances. Charismatic and religious figures often claim such talents, which assists in gaining revered and elevated status. Sometimes psychic healers channel their 'powers', for example through crystals tapping into energy sources, though research does not back this claim.

Out-of-body experiences (OBEs) and *near-death experiences* (NDEs) involve a perception of floating outside one's body and are linked, as people having NDEs often experience OBEs too. OBEs can be *parasomatic*, where individuals have a body other than their own or *asomatic*, where individuals perceive they have no body. Most OBEs happen in bed and are believed to transpire

Additional studies

- Braud & Schlitz (1988) found that galvanic skin responses were elevated when healers were asked to focus on pictures of patients unaware that this was occurring. This suggests a real biological effect to psychic healing.
- Blanke et al. (2005) found that stimulation of the right temporal-parietal brain area produced OBE simulations in participants with no history of OBEs, suggesting a biological basis to the phenomenon.
- Green (1968) found 75 per cent of OBEs occur with low arousal, such as when in bed, and 25 per cent occur with high arousal, such as when rock climbing. This suggests there are different sub-types of OBEs.
- Schwartz et al. (2001) found an accuracy level of 83 per cent in mediums compared to 36 per cent in controls, when interviewing a woman who had experienced six significant losses in ten years. The woman only answered 'yes' or 'no' to reduce the possibility of intuitive reasoning. This implies a genuine psychic effect.
- Bieschel & Schwartz (2007) found that mediums were better at 'reading' people who had lost loved ones than non-mediums, under conditions of strict experimental control, which suggests mediums can receive messages from the spirit world.

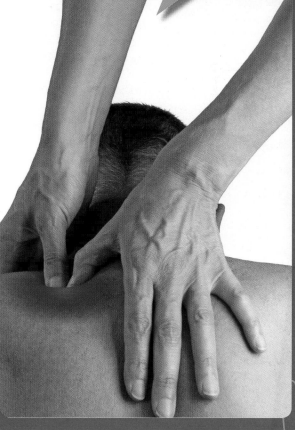

Positive evaluation

✔ Mollica (2005) argues that psychic healers benefit those in cultures where the practice is culturally familiar during catastrophes like earthquakes, as they provide 'psychological first-aid' that is not intrusive or anxiety-creating in the way that traditional medicine is.

✔ Psychic mediumship can be seen to perform an important part of the grieving process after the death of loved ones. Communicating between the spirits of the dead and their living human associates (whether genuine or not) often helps to reassure that the departed are 'at peace' and enables people to come to terms with their loss.

during a period between REM sleep and arousal, where sleep paralysis occurs and dream images combine with sensory input.

Psychic mediums exist cross-culturally, often as religious figures, like shaman, who claim to be intermediaries between the living and spirit worlds, carrying messages between the two, generally by altering their consciousness. They can help people come to terms with the death of loved ones. *Physical mediums* are visible to an audience, as at a séance, communicating to the spirit world through audible and visual figures, as well as raps. *Mental mediums* involve mediums using *clairvoyance*, where a medium sees a spirit, *clairaudience*, where a medium hears a spirit, *clairsentience*, where a medium senses the thoughts of a spirit and *trance mediumship*, where spirit communicators speak through a medium.

Negative evaluation

✗ Blackmore (1991) argues that NDEs are not evidence of 'life after death,' but instead inform more about the biological nature of consciousness and the brain.

✗ Lester (2005) reported that studies of psychic mediumship lack proper research design and elimination of error sources to be deemed valid.

✗ The Catholic Church, after a review of scientific literature, banned the practice of 'therapeutic touch,' demonstrating the practice to have little support even among religious believers.

▲ **Figure 12.4** Psychic healing involving physical contact is known as therapeutic touch

THE APPLICATION OF SCIENTIFIC METHOD IN PSYCHOLOGY

Replicability

Replication involves repeating studies under the same conditions to check reliability and validity of findings. This only occurs if research studies are written up fully in a designated manner. Fleischmann & Pons (1989) published research that appeared to verify the existence of cold fusion, whereby limitless energy could be created very cheaply. Because the research was written up in the required manner, other scientists were able to fully replicate their work where unfortunately they discovered that the phenomenon does not exist, presumably due to methodological error. Replication performs the important function of ensuring psychologists do not use practical applications in the real world until they have been shown to be based on solid, empirically-tested facts.

Description

The *scientific process* is a means of acquiring knowledge based on observable, measureable evidence, involving the generation and testing of hypotheses through *empirical methods*. These involve observations based on sensory experience, rather than thoughts and beliefs alone. A scientific fact is thus one that has been subjected to empirical testing by rigorous observation of phenomena and scientific facts must be explicable through theories that can be tested by empirical means. Science therefore requires predictions that are testable empirically, without bias or expectation of results, and under controlled conditions. In this manner theories can either be validated or falsified, though the challenge for Psychology is to achieve this in real-life settings.

Objectivity

Objectivity concerns observations made without bias, as science requires that research be performed without the application of distorted personal feelings and interpretations. Objectivity is an element of empiricism, where observations are made through sensory experience rather than biased viewpoints formed from expectation and desire. To lessen the chances of bias, standardised instructions, operational definitions of observed variables, physically defined measurements of performance and double-blind techniques are used. Bias in research, making findings subjective rather than objective, is generally unconscious rather than deliberate fraud. For example, when ganzfeld studies (which test for extra-sensory perception (ESP)) are performed by believers in ESP, results tend to confirm that ESP exists, but when performed by sceptics the exact same procedure tends to show that ESP does not exist.

Hypothesis testing

An integral part of the validation process is the notion of **falsifiability**, where hypotheses are tested and found to be false. This is achieved by replicating studies under the exact same testing conditions. Freud's psychodynamic theory is criticised for being unfalsifiable, as his interpretations of behaviour could not be shown to be untrue. For example, Freud argued that a person may behave in a certain way due to events in their childhood. If this was found to be so it is taken as evidence for the theory's validity. However, if it was found to be untrue it was still seen as supporting the theory through repression of the events due to their traumatic content.

Validating new knowledge and the role of peer review

Peer review is essential to scholarly communication and the verification process and involves the scrutiny of research papers by experts to determine scientific validity. Only when perceived as valid may papers be published in respected journals and thus peer review is regarded as a 'gatekeeper', lessening the possibility that unscientific research will be published and accepted as scientific fact. The process involves several experts being sent a copy of a research paper by a journal editor with several possible outcomes: accept the work unconditionally, accept if modifications are made, reject, but suggest revisions, reject outright.

Criticisms of peer review

- There are many organisations with a vested interest in ensuring that only certain research is published, for example, drug companies desiring studies published that suggest their products are effective. This puts great pressure on those involved in peer review to remain independent and unbiased.

- Research operates in a narrow social world that makes it difficult to peer review in an objective, unbiased way, due to jealousies or past differences, etc., that may occur between researchers.

- Reviewers have occasionally been accused of not validating research for publication so that their own work may be published first. Indeed, claims are even made of reviewers plagiarising research they were supposed to be scrutinising and passing it off as their own.

- Peer review can be slow, sometimes taking years to achieve.

▲ **Figure 13.1** Peer review involves scrutiny of research papers by experts before they are published

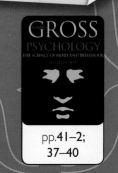

GROSS
PSYCHOLOGY
THE SCIENCE OF MIND AND BEHAVIOUR

pp.41–2;
37–40

DESIGNING PSYCHOLOGICAL INVESTIGATIONS

Implications of sampling strategies

Psychology uses several sampling methods, which have implications for bias and generalisation. *Random sampling* involves selection without bias, but does not guarantee unbiased samples, as for example an all-female sample could be randomly selected, incurring generalisation problems. *Opportunity sampling* makes use of people's availability, but results are often not generalisable, as only a certain 'type' of participants (e.g. shoppers) may have been selected. *Volunteer sampling* involves self-selection of participants and so requires little effort in obtaining, but volunteers are prone to demand characteristics and tend to be a certain 'type' and thus can be unrepresentative. *Systematic sampling* involves unbiased, equal-probability selection of every nth person and so findings are usually generalisable, though the sampling interval may hide a pattern that threatens randomness. *Stratified sampling* involves selection of participant groups according to their frequency in a target population. Individuals are selected for each group randomly, producing a fairly representative sample. If random sampling is not used it is called *quota sampling*, which is less representative.

Description

Different types of research method suit different research scenarios, each having their strengths and weaknesses:

- *Experiments* look for differences between testing groups and are most favoured where circumstances permit, being conducted under controlled conditions, allowing causality to be established and are easily replicated to confirm results. However, they lack external validity, though field and natural experiments are conducted in more naturalistic settings.

- *Correlations* show the intensity and direction of relationships between variables, identify areas worthy of experimental study, can sometimes be used where experiments would be unethical, but lack causality and cannot investigate non-linear relationships.

Issues of reliability

Reliability refers to consistency, with *internal reliability* concerning the extent to which something is consistent within itself and *external reliability* concerning the extent to which a measurement is consistent with other measurements of the same thing. *Test-re-test reliability* involves measurements being re-done over time to assess their stability, whilst *inter-rater reliability* refers to the degree to which different raters give consistent measurements of the same event, which is especially useful in observations.

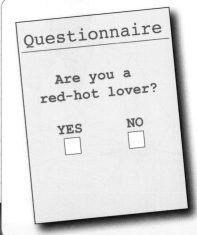

▲ **Figure 13.2** Questionnaires are vulnerable to idealised answers

Assessing and improving validity

Validity concerns accuracy. Internal validity involves whether an observed effect results from manipulation of an independent variable and can be improved by using random samples and standardised instructions and lessening of demand characteristics and investigator effects. External validity involves the extent to which results have ecological validity (generalisable to other settings), population validity (generalisable to other people) and historical validity (generalisable over time). Face validity assesses validity by examining the extent to which items a test appears to measure what it claims, while concurrent validity assesses validity by correlating scores on a test with another known valid test.

- *Self-reports*, such as questionnaires, interviews and surveys, gain information directly from participants, are relatively quick to perform, can identify areas worthy of more stringent study, but lack causality and are prone to idealised and socially desirable answers.

- *Observations* allow the viewing of natural behaviour and so have high external validity, but lack causality, are difficult to replicate and may lack inter-observer reliability.

- *Case studies* provide rich, detailed data on single persons or small groups and often give insight into unique circumstances, but lack causality and cannot be generalised.

Ethical considerations

The British Psychological Society's code of ethics is designed to protect participants from harm and loss of dignity.

- Informed consent involves participants receiving full details of research so that considered decisions can be made as to whether to participate. For those below 16 years and those incapable of informed consent, legal guardians must instead give consent.

- Presumptive consent involves gaining informed consent from similar non-participants who consent in place of the real participants, so that they remain naive of the hypothesis.

- Prior general consent is similar to presumptive consent, but involves the real participants consenting to being deceived, but without knowing how or when.

- Right to withdraw involves participants being informed that they can leave a study at any time, even by withdrawing data retrospectively.

- Deceit involves participants not being misled.

- Protection from harm involves participants leaving studies in the same mental and physical state that they entered them. Risk levels should not exceed those of everyday life.

- Debriefing involves participants being told all details of research, answering all their questions and being reassured about their performance.

DATA ANALYSIS AND REPORTING ON INVESTIGATIONS

Probability and significance

Probability involves deciding if results are significant, by giving a cut-off point that determines whether findings are beyond chance factors. Psychology uses a significance level of $p \leq 0.05$, giving a 95 per cent assurance of findings being beyond chance. In some instances, like testing new drugs, a more stringent level is used where $p \leq 0.01$, entailing a 99 per cent certainty of findings being significant. Type I errors occur when findings are accepted as significant, but are not, as the significance level was too low, while Type II errors occur when findings are accepted as insignificant, but are not, as the significance level was too high.

Appropriate selection of graphical representations

Graphs permit data to be displayed in an easily understandable, pictorial form, with different types for different circumstances. Graphs should be titled and axes labelled.

Bar charts display data in categories, represented on the horizontal x-axis as columns separated by spaces to show data is non-continuous, with frequencies on the y-axis.

Histograms also display data in categories, with values represented on the x-axis and frequencies on the y-axis. However, there are no spaces between columns, as the data is continuous.

Frequency polygons are similar to histograms in displaying continuous data, with the frequency polygon drawn from the midpoint tops of each column in a histogram. Two or more frequency distributions can be made on one graph.

Scattergrams show degree and direction of correlations between two co-variables.

Factors affecting choice of statistical test

Chi-squared is used when a difference is sought, an independent groups design is used and data is at least nominal, where it occurs as frequencies. The test is also used to assess correlations. *Mann-Whitney* is used when a difference is sought, an independent groups design is used and data is at least ordinal, where it occurs as ranks. *Wilcoxon signed-matched ranks* is used when a difference is sought, a repeated-measures design is used and data is at least ordinal. *Spearman's rho* is used when a correlation is sought, data is at least ordinal and occurs in pairs of scores from the same person or event.

Analysis and interpretation of qualitative data

Qualitative data is non-numerical, providing insight into feelings and thoughts, not possible with just numerical data. Underlying meanings are looked for, which can be subject to researcher bias. However, qualitative data can be converted into quantitative data, allowing it to be analysed in a more objective fashion. This involves converting data into categories, such as by **content analysis** where frequencies are counted of events, such as negative and positive words in text. Such data can then be presented descriptively by words and in tables and graphs as well as being analysed statistically.

▲ **Figure 13.3** When assessing new drugs a more stringent significance level of $p \leq 0.01$ is used

Conventions on reporting on psychological representations

Psychologists communicate effectively by publishing research in peer reviewed journals written in a prescribed manner to permit full replication, so that findings can be validated. The *title* should be clear, relevant and fully informative. The *table of contents* lists all sections with page numbers. The *abstract* consists of a concise statement of aims, hypotheses, methodology, results, conclusions and suggestions for future research. The *introduction* presents the theoretical background and previous research, contracting focus from an initial broader perspective down to an eventual narrower one. The *aims* and *hypotheses* are then quoted in an unambiguous, clear fashion, with justification for the direction of the experimental/alternative hypothesis being given. The *method* details all methodological requirements relating to the design and the participants, usually inclusive of ethical considerations, as well as materials, controls and the standardised procedure used. The *results* incur firstly as *descriptive statistics*, where measures of dispersion and central tendency are given and results summarised in appropriate graphs and tables, and secondly, as *inferential statistics*, where statistical tests are justified and outcome of analysis quoted in terms of the hypotheses. The *discussion* explains findings in terms of aims and hypotheses and evaluates them in terms of previous findings and theoretical aspects. Sources of error are identified and strategies suggested to resolve them, before implications of research and ideas for future research are presented. The *references* list all sources used, while the *appendices* detail standardised instructions, raw data and calculations, as well as other relevant information.

MAKING THE MOST OF EXAMINATIONS

The exams

Candidates may have attended all lessons, completed all work, revised hard and be motivated to do well. However, unless you perform well in your examinations you will not get what you deserve. Therefore, it is essential that you fully understand the exam process in order to succeed.

For the A2 qualification, students sit two papers:

1. Unit 3 focuses on topics in psychology, with eight questions, one each on the topics of *biological rhythms and sleep*, *perception*, *relationships*, *aggression*, *eating behaviour*, *gender*, *intelligence* and *cognition and development*. The exam lasts 90 minutes, so candidates will have around 30 minutes to answer each question.

2. Unit 4 divides into three sections: section A *psychopathology*, where candidates answer one question from a choice of four focused on *schizophrenia*, *depression*, *phobias* and *OCD*, section B *psychology in action*, where candidates answer one question from three focused on *media psychology*, *the psychology of addictive behaviour and anomalistic psychology* and section C *psychological research and scientific method* where candidates answer all questions. Unit 4 comprises 50 per cent of the total A2 marks, with 83 marks on offer (24 marks each for both sections A and B and 35 marks for section C). The exam lasts 2 hours.

Examination injunctions

Exam questions use examination injunctions, the type of words used in questions to inform students what kinds of answers are required. An understanding of these terms allows you to confidently write exam answers that match the requirements of the questions and thus gain access to all the marks on offer:

AO1 – *Identify* means simply to name, no other description is required. *Define* involves explaining what is meant by.

Outline means give brief details without explanation. *Describe* means give a detailed account without explanation.

AO2 – *Give* means to show awareness of. *Explain* means to give a clear account of why and how something is so. *Evaluate* means to assess the value or effectiveness of. *Discuss* means to give a reasoned balanced account (including descriptive material). *Apply* means to explain how something can be used.

Types of exam questions

At A2 questions occur in varying formats requiring certain types of answers. The Unit 3 questions and those pertaining to sections A and B of Unit 4 generally occur as two different types.

First, there will be essay style 'whole' questions that require answers that are continuous, such as 'outline and evaluate research into psychic healing'. Such questions will be worth 24 marks each, with 8 marks available for description of knowledge and 16 marks available for evaluation and analysis.

Secondly there will be parted questions, which collectively add up to 24 marks each, again with 8 marks available for description of knowledge and 16 marks available for evaluation and analysis, but such questions will occur in discrete parts requiring separate answers. The marks for each discrete part will occur in brackets after the question. Such parted questions may focus collectively on one element of a topic, for example upon biological rhythms, such as, a) 'Outline one example of an infradian rhythm' [4 marks], b) 'Outline and evaluate the disruption of biological rhythms [20 marks] or could focus on several elements from a topic, for example biological rhythms and sleep disorders, for example, a) 'Outline one example of an infradian rhythm [4 marks], b) 'Outline and evaluate explanations for insomnia' [20 marks].

All Unit 3 questions will additionally require material on *issues, debates and approaches* (IDA) to gain appropriate credit. The Unit 4 section C questions will occur as shorter-answer questions based on psychological research and scientific method. Stimulus material may be provided upon which candidates are expected to base their answers. Most questions here will require short answers, worth a few marks, exactly how many being stated in brackets after the question, giving some indication of how much material is to be supplied to get full marks. For example 'Identify one extraneous variable that might occur and explain how this could be dealt with' [4 marks]. There may be longer-answer questions too, requiring fuller, more detailed answers, such as 'With reference to the data in the table, outline and discuss the findings of this investigation' [10 marks].

▲ **Figure 14.1**

Revision strategies

Many students incorrectly see revision as something done immediately before examinations. Although pre-examination revision is important, revision is something that should be incorporated into your studies throughout the course and indeed is an integral part of the learning process. At the end of studying each element of a topic you should revise the material to develop a deeper understanding and to check that all material has been covered and is fully understood. The best way to achieve this is to engage with the material, for example by reading through notes/worksheets, etc., highlighting the main points. Make use of available textbooks to further elaborate your knowledge; better candidates will be making use of more than just one source of information. After this, attempt an exam-type question to assess your level of knowledge and understanding and also to familiarise yourself with the kind of questions you may ultimately be asked. Such questions can be accessed on the AQA website by reference to previous exam questions and to sample questions. These also include advice on what types of things to include in your answer. Over time make sure that you include all types of possible questions in your revision, not just those concerning outlining and describing, but also those requiring explanations and evaluations.

How to revise exam questions

When first practising exam questions you will need all learning materials to hand, like notes and handouts. Ensure you fully understand the requirements of the question from the command words and know how much to write by reference to the number of marks on offer. Make a plan in numbered bullet point form and then have a go at writing your answer, only giving yourself the same amount of time as in the real exam (about 1 minute and 15 seconds per mark). You will probably have to refer to learning materials when writing your answer, but as you become familiar with this method, you will increasingly be able to write answers without them. A good way to achieve this is to read through relevant materials first, then put them away before writing your answer.

Making a revision timetable

Before commencing pre-exam revision you will need a revision timetable. This is best achieved by having morning, afternoon and evening sessions for each day. You can then use this as a template for each separate week of revision. For each of your subjects make a list of the topics you need to revise. Then, using a pencil at first, slot in the topics, making sure that you first block out any sessions that are not available due to other commitments. It is probably best to initially revise subjects and topics that will be examined first. A revision programme has to be achievable, so ensure that there are a few spare slots each week to use if any planned revision sessions do not occur. When you have finally got all the topics entered, colour them in using a different colour for each subject. Put your revision timetable up on a wall and tick off sessions as you go. You might even give a copy to a parent so they can police you and make sure sessions get done. Having a revision timetable like this increases confidence that revision can be completed, which in turn increases motivation to actually revise.

Pre-examination revision

All topics need to be revised, including ones you find difficult, as they have an equal chance of being on the exam paper. Ensure you have listed all the topics you have studied and have all materials necessary for revising each topic. Find somewhere comfortable to revise away from distractions. Make sure that everything you need for revising, like tidying up your desk, is done before revision starts. It is easy to spend all the designated revision time on distraction activities, like sorting out books and sharpening pencils. About 90 minutes a session will be best, using the revision method you have practised all year, namely, reading through necessary materials, highlighting important points and using previous exam questions to construct answers. Give yourself a planned reward for completing revision sessions, be it chocolate or a favourite TV programme. Revising in a constant, organised way like this is the best route to maximising exam performance.

▲ Figure 14.2